Offer Them Christ

Offer Them Christ

Christian Mission for the Twenty-First Century

WILLIAM M. PICKARD JR.

PROVIDENCE HOUSE PUBLISHERS
Franklin, Tennessee

Printed in the United States of America

02   01   00   99   98   1   2   3   4   5

Library of Congress Catalog Card Number: 98-65599

ISBN: 1-57736-090-7

Cover design by Gary Bozeman

*Unless otherwise indicated, all Scripture references are from the
Revised Standard Version of the Bible.*

PROVIDENCE HOUSE PUBLISHERS
238 Seaboard Lane • Franklin, Tennessee 37067
800-321-5692

To
MY WIFE
Mary Ann

OUR CHILDREN
Susan and Lorenzo, Henry and Frances,
Marshall, Jamie and Barbara, and Wes and Susan

AND OUR GRANDCHILDREN
Gerald, Michael, Susana, Tom, Patricia,
Wesley, Mary Ann, James, Will, and Jacob

One Solitary Life

He was born in an obscure village. He worked in a carpenter shop until He was thirty. He then became an itinerant preacher. He never held an office. He never had a family or owned a house. He didn't go to college. He had no credentials but himself. He was only thirty-three when the public turned against him. His friends ran away. He was turned over to his enemies and went through the mockery of a trial. He was nailed to a cross between two thieves. While He was dying, his executioners gambled for his clothing, the only property He had on earth. He was laid in a borrowed grave. Nineteen centuries have come and gone, and today He is the central figure of the human race. All the armies that ever marched, all the navies that ever sailed, all the parliaments that ever sat, and all the kings that ever reigned have not affected the life of man on this earth as much as that One Solitary Life.

—Author Unknown

CONTENTS

FOREWORD

RECENTLY, A DRAMATIC RELIGIOUS DEVELOPMENT HAS TAKEN PLACE before our very eyes in America. It is the fact of religious pluralism. There was a time when world religions were a phenomena related only to distant lands. Christianity and Judaism we knew, but other faiths were remote to us, subjects for scholars and missionaries.

How this has changed. Muslims are the third largest religious group in the United States. Mosques are now found in all our larger cities, along with Hindu temples, affording a place of worship for their adherents among us. Buddhists are present in increasing numbers, while bearded and turban-crowned Sikhs are not an unfamiliar sight on our streets. These changes strike traditional American Christians and Jews with both surprise and dismay.

At the same time there has also appeared a failure of nerve on the part of many Christians and an undercutting of missionary incentive. So the questions are posed: Are not all religions essentially the same? What is unique about Jesus Christ? Why force our religion upon others? At the very same time, the role of Jesus is called into question by some within the church itself.

It is with this new situation that this book is concerned. Some of the questions just raised are often distorted and need to be phrased and answered in a different way. This volume argues the case for Jesus Christ in a new and compelling manner.

Dr. Pickard has for some years given careful attention to and reflection upon these matters. He reviews the various historic approaches to

Christology—examining the biblical claims of Jesus as the Way, the Truth, and the Life. He studies with meticulous care the problems which arise in long-standing debates about who Jesus was and is. This is not theology made easy, but theology made clear. Dr. Pickard unashamedly states his own conclusion in what he terms "Person Christology." The reader is advised to follow his argument with care. His stand is neither narrowly focused nor contentious nor exclusivist.

His chapter, "The Saviour" is particularly appealing. In his argument for our personal encounter with Jesus, Dr. Pickard uses the metaphor of "counseling therapy" as a paradigm. The therapist, in order to relate effectively with the patient, must have certain essential qualities: authenticity, sensitivity, empathy, acceptance, stability, ability to direct the perplexed toward meaning, and so on. Jesus possesses precisely such qualities in remarkable measure, well deserving of Isaiah's phrase for the Messiah: "Wonderful Counselor." He is the one who confronts us, and even today transforms people who stand in need of salvation with the guilts, anxieties, and fears that attach to stressful living. All of this transcends the issue of religious pluralism as such. The focus is not on Christianity, but Christ. Pickard illustrates this approach through the work of the modern missionary witness, the late Dr. E. Stanley Jones.

Dr. Pickard himself served as a missionary in the Philippines, and he is acquainted with other areas too, particularly India. Since I am myself a former missionary to India, I know the topic is crucial. My own doctoral work has been in this field and I recall how much my late father-in-law, Dr. E. Stanley Jones, was concerned about it. My recent exchange with the late Bishop Lesslie Newbigin made clear his own deep concern as well.

Dr. Pickard taught missions and related subjects for years to college students, and he is active in evangelism as General Secretary of the United Christian Ashram movement. He unashamedly and persuasively appeals to men and women today as he "offers them Christ."

James K. Mathews
Bishop, The United Methodist Church

PREFACE

THE TITLE OF THIS BOOK COMES FROM JOHN WESLEY'S ADMONITION to Francis Asbury as Asbury set sail for America in 1771. Asbury sought to carry out the admonition, "Offer them Christ," with great commitment, riding more than 200,000 miles on horseback across the "new world" proclaiming the gospel.

The book has been many years in the making—in fact, more than twenty in the actual writing. It is the fruit of more than sixty years of Christian ministry, reaching back to before I was born. From her early childhood my mother wanted to be a missionary. As a young lady she married a Methodist preacher, my father. She never got to the mission field in person. But vicariously she did go through her participation in and support of the Woman's Society of Christian Service of the Methodist Church and through two of her sons. My brother, Dr. Raleigh Henry Pickard, spent thirty-two years as a medical missionary in India. I spent sixteen years as an evangelistic missionary in the Philippines. My sister, Eleanor Pickard Luce, married a professor in a Christian college, and my youngest brother, Dr. Samuel David Pickard, served as an ordained minister of the United Methodist Church in Alabama for over forty years. We all grew up on the message of world missions and particularly on the devotional books of the missionary, Dr. E. Stanley Jones.

My high school, college, and seminary years were spent not only under the inspiration of my mother and father, but also under the influence of the late Walter Russell Lambuth, long-time missionary and Methodist bishop John R. Mott, Sherwood Eddy, E. Stanley Jones, and a host of other missionaries and missionary statesmen. By the time I reached seminary I was feeling very strongly the call to be a missionary.

Indeed, increasingly I began to feel that not to be a missionary, whether in my home state of Alabama or in some faraway country overseas, was not to be a part of the church. In time the very definition of the church came to be found in Acts 1:8: "You shall be my witnesses in Jerusalem, in Judea, and Samaria, and to the ends of the earth." I came to see that actually the church of Jesus Christ does not *have* a mission. Rather it *is* God's mission in the world or else it is not the church. Without being God's mission in the world, it might be a very fine organization—promoting and doing good things—but it would not be the church. There are many fine organizations—civic clubs, fraternal orders, etc. But they are not the church. The thing that distinguishes the church from all other good organizations is that it is God's mission in the world. Jesus said, as he instituted the church, "You shall be my witnesses in Jerusalem, in Judea, and Samaria, and to the ends of the earth." You shall be *my* witnesses.

As a young man, my ordination as an elder in the Methodist Church and subsequently my acceptance as a missionary in the Philippines set me on a course that has inspired me and absorbed all of my thought and energy across the years. My missionary career came directly on the heels of the great Centenary Celebration in Methodism, which set world missions at the center as the all-controlling task of the church. It inspired thousands with the motto created by John R. Mott and the student Volunteer movement: "The Evangelization of the World in this Generation."

It came as a considerable shock to me, therefore, after several years on the mission field to discover a strain of theology developing which questioned the uniqueness of Jesus Christ, calling it a "myth."[1] To me, they were questioning the foundation of the Christian faith—the Incarnation.

Over the years there had been a growing awareness of other religions in our world in what we are calling today the rise of "religious pluralism." The rapid development of technology in the areas of communication and transportation has created a kind of "global community" and made us more conscious of persons who are adherents of other religions. As Christians we should of course relate to these persons of other faiths in a positive, friendly way, respecting them and their religions. But what I found some theologians doing was not only stressing friendly relationships with persons of other faiths, but out of a sense of guilt that Christians have sometimes been arrogant and not respectful of persons of other faiths and their religions, insisting that we must now view all religions as essentially the same, one as good as another. I realized that if this relativistic ideology should prevail, then indeed the Christian mission to which I had given my life was over, and in fact, I had been wrong all along to be in mission.

After five years on the mission field, I spent a year on furlough in graduate study looking at these issues, and eventually after another term of service in the mission field, wrote my doctoral dissertation on the subject. At the time of writing the dissertation, the central issue was being posed as the question of whether there is a continuity or discontinuity between the Christian faith and other religions. Is there something quite unique in the Christian faith, or is there a common denominator for all the religions? The title of the dissertation, which was in the discipline of Systematic Theology, was "The Doctrine of Man as a Clue to the Continuity-Discontinuity Debate in Twentieth Century Missiology."

The research and study for this dissertation and for all else that has gone into the writing of this book, together with the continuing challenge of religious pluralism today, has led me to some fundamental convictions which are set forth here. We certainly must do away with the arrogance that has inhered in both the so-called "exclusivistic" and "inclusivistic" positions in missiology which have plagued Christians across the years. But we cannot give up the belief in the uniqueness of Jesus Christ.

With this conviction, I became convinced that we must find a way to maintain the absolute uniqueness of Jesus Christ which is neither narrowly dogmatic nor in any way casts aspersion on the other religious traditions in the world. Such a statement of the uniqueness of Jesus must be both compelling and also intellectually respectable, gaining the respect, though not necessarily the agreement, of theologians of all religious traditions. It cannot be simply a dogmatic assertion. For I began to feel that if it is true, there must be some evidence of its truth. And I would have to find this.

This book approaches the matter by taking two important steps. First, it centers mission in Christology and Christology in the Resurrection.[2] The risen Jesus Christ actually living in person today is made the center of Christology. The writer assumes the traditional Incarnational Christology—the virgin birth, the deity of Jesus Christ, the atoning death on the cross, etc., but quickly moves to focus on the risen person, Jesus Christ living today, who he is and what he does. If Jesus Christ is divine as well as human, as Christians believe, then the Christology developed here follows. The author deals with this affirmation of the Incarnation in terms of what are fact-claims or beliefs and how they may be reasonably substantiated, though not necessarily proven in the strictest sense scientifically. We stress that this focus on Jesus, risen from the grave and living today is essential if we are to affirm the uniqueness of Jesus Christ and yet avoid the arrogance and the superiority complex of dogmatic "exclusivism" or "inclusivism." A rationale for this claim is developed.

Correspondingly, salvation (the major issue in interreligious dialogue), is seen in the Christian context to be the direct result of an interpersonal encounter with the risen, living person, Jesus Christ, and not merely as is commonly viewed, the result of a formal verbal profession of faith, though profession of faith is important and indeed essential. Salvation through faith, a cardinal Christian doctrine, is given deeper meaning. For faith, often erroneously identified with simple belief, is actually an interpersonal relationship that is basically trust at a deep interpersonal level. Salvation, the actual inner transformation, comes about through a dynamic interpersonal encounter with the living person, Jesus Christ. This is salvation by faith or through faith.

This view of salvation as a dynamic process which actually takes place in the context of interpersonal encounter with Jesus Christ is developed in terms of the paradigm of what can and does take place in human interpersonal encounter through counseling therapy. Recent study and practice show that the important thing in successful counseling therapy is not the techniques or methods used, but the actual dynamic interfacing and interpersonal encounter of the therapist or counselor with the client. Furthermore, the key factor here is not, as many assume, the skill and the methods used by the therapist, but the quality of his or her personhood. The healing, the change in the client, the "cure" is the direct result of the interpersonal dynamics that take place between therapist and client. A disturbed, fractured person comes into relationship with a well trained, mature, caring, loving person, and the interpersonal influence of one person on the other is what causes the change in the client, if and when it happens. It is a mystery, but is confirmed over and over. It is what Martin Buber calls the "I–Thou" encounter and relationship.

This principle is applied to the dynamic encounter of the distraught troubled sinner with the perfect, all-sufficient living person, Jesus Christ. It is through this dynamic interpersonal encounter with Jesus Christ that salvation takes place. Isaiah 9:6 says of the Messiah: ". . . his name will be called Wonderful Counselor, Mighty God, Everlasting Father, Prince of Peace."

Using the phrase "Wonderful Counselor" and taking it seriously, the author shows, first, that in the same way that a mentally or socially or psychologically ill person may experience "healing" through a dynamic interpersonal relationship with a well-trained, mature, empathetic counselor, so a spiritually ill person, a sinner, may experience complete transformation of life through a genuine interpersonal encounter with the Supreme Person, Jesus Christ, who is living today and who will encounter and transform if we surrender to him. What actually happens to and in the person is a dynamic change, a transformation of the person on the inside as a result of the interpersonal encounter with Jesus Christ. This understanding of Christian salvation is essential if we are to maintain the essence of the Christian faith and the uniqueness of Jesus Christ without arrogance in a world of religious pluralism. Explaining why and how this is true is part of the purpose of this book.

The second step is to undergird this Christology with an adequate ontology that makes the Christology reasonable and compelling. Gerald O'Collins is right when he says

> Every Christology must be properly philosophical. Any serious discussion of Jesus Christ brings us into the deep water where we confront the final meaning of reality and the most basic needs of man. An undertow of philosophical issues tugs at Christology from start to finish.[3]

With this in mind, I seek to provide a philosophical base by developing what I call a Person-Nonperson ontology. Utilizing and modifying both "Boston Personalism" and "Cartesian Dualism," I establish an ontology which supports Person Christology in terms of the final meaning of reality. In this way I believe that I come out with a sound theology, which answers adequately the contemporary challenge which religious pluralism poses to belief in the uniqueness of Jesus Christ. Likewise, I seek to establish the validity and the urgency of the Christian mission in the world today. Other things the book does are:

First, it seeks to establish the validity of holding absolutes in an age of religious relativism. It presents Jesus Christ as the Absolute—the Way, the Truth, and the Life and gives a rationale for this position.

Second, it presents an approach to interreligious dialogue. Such dialogue will be extremely important in the twenty-first century The approach presented here is based on the "Round Table Conference" developed by E. Stanley Jones. This approach does not center in studying and exploring religious beliefs in order to compare and to understand the religions—the academic quest. Though such an approach is a valid part of dialogue, it is not the approach presented in this book. Rather, the approach presented here centers in exploring beliefs and practices as they relate to, and mesh with, daily living—the existential, personal quest. Such dialogue is open-ended.

Third, it presents an approach to the understanding of truth, which clarifies the words *true* and *truth* in religious discourse, particularly in religious dialogue. As we confront the issues involved in religious pluralism, the question of truth is paramount. What do we mean by the word *truth*? Is there truth in all or in any of the religions? Is truth possible? Can we know the truth? Is there a true religion? What would a "true" religion be? We explore these questions in chapter two.

Fourth, it presents in chapter six a specific example of Christian world mission and evangelism in an age of religious pluralism, based on the principles set forth here and carried out quite successfully in the most religiously plural part of the world, the subcontinent of India. This specific example is the E. Stanley Jones model for world evangelization.

ACKNOWLEDGMENTS

A BOOK OF THIS NATURE IS ALWAYS A GROUP ENDEAVOR. MANY persons have contributed to what I have written. I am indebted to so many that I cannot possibly mention all the names here. However, I must express appreciation to several colleagues and friends who have done me the favor of reading the manuscript at various stages in its development and have made invaluable suggestions: Dr. Roger Dick Johns, my colleague at Huntingdon College; Dr. Theodore H. Runyon and Dr. Luke Johnson of Candler School of Theology, Emory University; Dr. Arthur Glasser of Fuller Theological Seminary; Dr. Glenn Bannister, counseling psychologist, Montgomery, Alabama; Dr. J. T. Seamands, professor of missions, Asbury Theological Seminary; Bishop James K. Mathews, former missionary to India (son-in-law of E. Stanley Jones) and bishop in the United Methodist Church, and his wife, Eunice Jones Mathews; Dr. Gordon Hunter of Toronto, Canada; Dr. John Sanders, Oak Hills Bible College, Bemudgi, Minnesota; my former professor and now Bishop Mack B. Stokes of the United Methodist Church; and Dr. William Abraham, Perkins School of Theology, Southern Methodist University.

Of course, as will be abundantly clear, the one to whom I am most indebted for the content of this book is the late Dr. E. Stanley Jones, missionary to India and the world, from whom I have learned the most about the missionary task today. Also I want to express appreciation to the United Christian Ashrams Ministry, founded by Dr. E. Stanley Jones, for encouragement and allowing me time away from the office to complete the work. However, I take full responsibility for all the mistakes and short-comings you will find in this book.

Last, but far from least, the person I am without any doubt the most indebted to and most grateful for is my wife, Mary Ann Martin Pickard. Not only has she sustained me and participated with me for more than fifty years during my ministry and missionary career, she has made many valuable suggestions in writing the manuscript. She has laboriously and cheerfully typed and retyped, including over a dozen revisions, every word of the manuscript into a computer. If the truth were really known, this is much more her book than mine. I owe her a debt of gratitude I can never repay.

Chapter One
OFFER THEM CHRIST

THE WAY

THE CHRISTIAN FAITH IS AND ALWAYS HAS BEEN AN EVANGELISTIC and missionary faith. The goal of world evangelization is as inherent to the Christian faith as the Cross. It is in fact based on the Cross. Christians believe that Christ died for the entire world. The theology of the Cross is inherently a missionary theology. Not only the Great Commission, to go into all the world, but the entire witness of scripture makes this clear. The letters of Paul and the Gentile mission set forth in the book of Acts focus on moving out to evangelize the world. Whether the focus is on the being and essence of Jesus Christ—"If I be lifted up I will draw all men unto me"—or on going out (the Great Commission), Christianity is inherently a missionary faith. The Christian mission brought Europe under the sway of Christianity in the first few centuries of the Christian era. This rapid growth of Christianity in the first few centuries was followed by several centuries of consolidation, development of the creeds of the church, etc. The missionary expansion in the eighteenth, nineteenth, and twentieth centuries has taken Christianity into almost every part of the world.

This missionary expansion of Christianity is an amazing story, which has been told in many places and in many ways. As we enter the twenty-first century there is no sign that this missionary effort is slackening. The more traditional "mainline" denominations and some local churches in many cases may be losing some of their zeal for mission and evangelism. Some have turned almost exclusively to liberation theology, focusing on social, economic, and political issues. Though "liberation" is certainly a valid and important part of Christian mission, to focus entirely on it is to be off center. Others have turned inward, focusing on themselves with emphasis on structure, program, smoothly functioning administration, equal representation (ethnic, racial, age, gender) on governing boards, etc. Still others have become primarily social clubs with little or no interest in missionary outreach.

However, this retrenchment in some so-called mainline denominations and individual churches has been more than offset by the missionary outreach of "faith" missions, Pentecostals, independent and other more evangelical churches, Roman Catholic, Protestant, and Eastern Orthodox. Thousands of missionaries are going out and thousands of dollars are being invested in missionary outreach. In 1900 there were 62,000 "foreign" (expatriate) missionaries at work in the world. By 1970 the number had quadrupled to 240,000. In the next twenty-eight years another 60,000 have been added, bringing the total in 1998 to over 400,000. In 1900, $200 million was spent on "foreign missions." By 1970 the figure had increased over tenfold to $3 billion, and twenty years later to the amazing total of almost $12 billion annually. It is expected to be $60 billion by 2025. The number of Christians in Africa increased from 8,756,400 in 1900 to 329,882,000 in 1998, and is expected to reach 700 million by 2025.[1] The world mission of the Christian church is alive and well. There is certainly no abatement in the zeal of Christians to evangelize the world.

Yet, there is a rising tide of Christian theology today which is calling into question this entire Christian missionary enterprise.[2] This theology is telling us in effect that the mission of the Christian church from the beginning has been a mistake based on a gross misunderstanding of religion. This faulty or distorted understanding of Christianity, with the missionary outreach involved, according to these theologians, has been greatly augmented by the explosion of technology and the colonial expansion of the West in the seventeenth, eighteenth, nineteenth, and twentieth centuries. Twentieth-century studies in religion, according to these theologians, have brought a better understanding of the origin, history, and inherent nature of the religious life of mankind. We can now see our historical errors, according to this view, and must repent of our alliance with western colonialism and our exploitation of non-Western peoples including the attempt to destroy their religions and to westernize their cultures. We must give up our Christian "colonialist" expansion, accept the validity of all religions, and cease our efforts at world evangelization.

We reject this view completely, though we certainly recognize and repent of all Christian complicity with colonialism, as we will point out below. Christianity has at times been allied with colonialism, and we are ashamed of this record. The problem has been the institutional focus of Christian mission, the focus on religion rather than on the person, Jesus Christ. The first Christians did not see themselves, nor were they seen as starting a new religion. In fact, in the beginning and until Gentiles began joining the movement, all of them were Jewish in their religion and remained so. They simply called themselves, and were known as, the people of "the Way." They followed a "*way*," the Way of Jesus. This, I suggest, is what it means to be a Christian. Christian mission for the twenty-first century must be based on this understanding.

The movement within Christian theology toward complete religious relativism is rooted in the history of the past one hundred years. The rapid growth of the Christian mission in the nineteenth century produced a reaction among leaders of other religions. A call for the recognition of a place for all religions came at the "Parliament of World Religions" in Chicago, 1893. By the turn of the century, this call was being heard by more and more missiologists and other theologians. A number of factors may be noted as contributing to this growth of religious relativism. First, there was the rise to ascendancy in the nineteenth and early twentieth centuries of the so-called "liberal" theology stemming mainly from the work of Friedrick Schleiermacher. Second, the social gospel emphasis growing out of the work of Walter Rauschenbush and liberal theology in general turned attention away from the Christian gospel as it relates to "eternal salvation" and focused attention more on relieving man's plight in this world. Third, there was the impact of growing rationalism and the advance of the focus on science, some of which began questioning religious faith. Fourth, there was the impact of the uncertainty about Jesus growing out of the nineteenth century "quest of the historical Jesus." Fifth, there was a rapid growth of relativism in general under the influence of Ernst Troeltsch and others. Sixth, there was the emerging twentieth century focus on the secular world. Seventh, there was the beginning of the emergence of a world community as a result of industrial and technological advances in communication and transportation. Eighth, there was the beginning of serious academic study of world religions in the universities. Ninth, the so-called "History of Religions School of Theology" began to exert considerable influence on missiology.

As these factors played an increasing role in the thinking of the population in general and in the thinking of missiologists in particular, there came an increase in emphasis on the question of the relationship of Christianity to other religions, with a focus on similarities and common elements as well as differences. Also there developed a steady erosion of the emphasis on the uniqueness of Jesus Christ and a consequent shift toward the ideology of religious relativism. This shift was resisted by many and occasioned heated debate, but it has persisted throughout the twentieth century and may be observed as a kind of progressive development.

First, there came what might be called the "Recognize the good in other religions" stage. A serious study of other religions showed clearly that there were at least some good elements in some of them. Honesty and fairness demanded that this be recognized. Second, there was the "Utilize the good in other religions" stage. The good in other religions could be a point of contact for evangelization. Third, there developed the Praeparatia Evangelica stage. In this stage many Christians began to view the good in other religions as not only usable, but as a positive preparation for the gospel. Other religions came to be seen by many, in the words of Paul concerning the Jewish law (Gal. 3:24) as "schoolmasters" to lead persons to Christ.

The fourth stage was what might be called the "Crown" stage. Some missiologists began seeing other religions not just as preparation for Christianity, but as embryonic versions of Christianity to be developed into full expressions of the Christian faith. In 1913 J. N. Farquhar published a book titled *The Crown of Hinduism,*[3] which spoke of the Christian faith "crowning" or completing Hinduism and other non-Christian religions.

Of course there were strong voices raised in opposition to these developments, and at the Jerusalem meeting of the International Missionary Council in 1928 the debate was lively. The issue as it was posed at that time was: Is there a continuity or a discontinuity between other religions and the Christian faith? Conservatives who held to the complete uniqueness of the Christian faith insisted that there was a total discontinuity. The more liberal missiologists rejected this complete discontinuity, insisting that there was a continuity which they sought to show. It was the heyday of liberalism in theology as a whole across both Europe and America, and the liberal approach gradually gained ascendancy, with the consequent move toward more religious relativism.

The present writer takes issue with this development. Indeed, he insists that the question is not one of continuity or discontinuity. If we focus on religions as such, there is some of both, depending on the aspects of the religions we are looking at. The focus in this book is not phenomenological or doctrinal, but rather existential. It is a focus on the living person, Jesus Christ in relation to other persons and to all institutions, including the institution we call religion.

In the first half of the twentieth century this move toward full recognition of other religions came to its most complete expression in the report of a group of laymen who in the 1930s on their own initiative made an extensive study of the foreign missionary enterprise. The report was written largely by the philosopher William Ernest Hocking who was chairman of the Inquiry Committee. It was published under the title, *Re-Thinking Missions, A Laymen's Inquiry After One Hundred Years*.[4] In the report, Hocking points out that there are three possibilities as regards the relationship of religions to each other. One is what he calls "radical displacement." This was the position of most Christians up to that time, namely that Christianity would replace all the other religions of the world. Second, is "syncretism" which means taking elements from all the religions and merging them into one. Third, is "reconception" in which all religions live side by side, with each religion recognizing and respecting all the others, but in process, reconceiving its own "essence" and thus making a distinctive contribution to the whole of mankind's religious life. Hocking chose this last alternative and sought to develop it. It is a thoroughly philosophical approach and is the forerunner of the contemporary "universal theology of religion" being advocated by many, which declares all religions to be essentially on the same footing.[5]

A reaction to *Rethinking Missions* came with Hendrik Kraemer's book *The Christian Message in a Non-Christian World*.[6] First published in 1938, this book was written as a study document for the 1938 meeting of the International Missionary Council at Madras, India. It declared again the uniqueness of the Christian gospel (called "Biblical Realism"), stressed complete discontinuity, and drew a heated response from the liberal missiologists of the day. Clearly, theological liberalism was in the ascendancy in 1938 and Kraemer seemed to be out of step with the modern world. Considerable discussion ensued with Kraemer being accused of turning the clock back fifty years to the nineteenth century. The next thirty years saw an extensive discussion spoken of as the "Hocking-Kraemer debate" or the "continuity-discontinuity debate."

Though much has been written since 1938, it is important to note that the polarity expressed by the two books *Re-Thinking Missions* and *The*

Christian Message In a Non-Christian World has persisted, and forms the core of the theological debate concerning missions today. The "universal theologists" have, in the main, taken up the legacy of *Re-Thinking Missions* with its focus on religion, pluralism, and relativism. The "evangelical" missiologists have, in the main, taken up the legacy of *The Christian Message in a Non-Christian World* with its focus on Jesus Christ as "the Way," as the Absolute. If one wishes to go more deeply into the background of the issues as they are posed today, he/she should read these two books.

THE CASE FOR A THEOLOGY BASED ON RELATIVISM

With this brief survey, we will now look at the reasons being given for the move to relativism on the part of a number of missiologists, which means in my judgment the surrender of the claim to the uniqueness of Jesus Christ, and the abandonment in effect of the Christian world mission. To do this we need first to distinguish carefully between religious pluralism as a cultural fact, which is cited as the basic rationale for the shift to religious relativism, and religious pluralism as an ideology. Religious pluralism as a cultural phenomenon is simply a fact, though in recent years, due to a shrinking world, it is being experienced in a new way. Different religious beliefs and traditions have grown up in different cultures so there are many "religions." However, this fact of a plurality of religious traditions in our world tells us nothing, except that there is a plurality of religious traditions in the world. If we move beyond this simple fact, as some theologians are doing, and begin to draw conclusions based on religious pluralism, we quickly move over into treating pluralism as an ideology. An ideology is a conceptual system on the basis of which certain facts and beliefs are interpreted and certain conclusions drawn. This is what religious pluralism has become for many today. Because there are many religions in the world, each with its own beliefs and standards, it is concluded that there can be no one correct or true religion and therefore no one standard of value or of right and wrong. Such an ideological position assumes that the only absolute is that there are no absolutes, which is of course a contradiction in terms. Persons holding to this ideology are urging us to give up the claim of Christian uniqueness as being a "myth" in order that we may not offend adherents of other religions (Hick and Knitter, *The Myth of Christian Uniqueness*, cited above).

Therefore, we must carefully distinguish between the fact of a plurality of religious traditions in our world and this ideology of religious pluralism.

We must also remember that an ideology is always based on certain presuppositions about reality that are assumed, but not proven. The writers advocating theological relativism would have us believe that since the study of the history of religion has shown that religious pluralism and historical relativism are simply facts of life, therefore any absolute in the realm of religious faith is impossible. They would tell us that theology based on the uniqueness of Christianity or of Jesus Christ is founded on a mere belief, a confessional affirmation, and therefore is simply speculation, whereas theology based on religious relativism is founded on historical fact and therefore is firm. We need to look carefully at this claim. One problem with this argument is that it fails to recognize that confessional beliefs are in themselves as much facts of history as are the religions themselves. The only question is, "What conclusion can we draw from either of these facts?" The conclusions we draw will be based not only on the facts themselves, but also on the presuppositions we bring to the facts. These ultimate presuppositions are of necessity unproven assumptions. In other words, they are an ideology.

For example, the presupposition that because all historical religions are relative, there can be no absolutes in religion, is based on two prior unproven assumptions: (1) That collective human experience (known as culture) sets the limits of what can and cannot be. Human beings collectively are the measure of all things. (2) That cultural relativity implies ethical relativity and renders any kind of absolutes in religion impossible. The assumption is that because the moral standards in all religions are different and therefore relative, there can be no absolute norm or standard applicable to all. This assumption that *what is*, determines absolutely *what can be* is clearly based on the presupposition of mechanical determinism. Such determinism is not only unproven, but as a theory is being seriously questioned even in the realm of the physical world by modern physics, particularly by the Heisenberg theory of indeterminism. In other words, theology based on religious relativism is just as surely based on unproven assumptions as is theology based on any confessional belief. We need to recognize the truth of the old adage: "What's sauce for the goose is sauce for the gander." If the Christian is not permitted by the rules of the game to declare on the basis of his belief in the Incarnation—that Jesus Christ as a living person is the unique and absolute standard and criterion—then the relativistic theologian is not allowed by the same rules to declare relativism to be the unique and absolute standard and criterion. Neither can he pick an arbitrary absolute such as "God," or the "Real" (Hick) or "Mystery" (Samartha), while disallowing others to take as their absolute Jesus Christ as the revelation of God.

This is the fallacy in John Hick's "theocentric" approach. He assumes that "God" or the "Real" is an unquestioned reality, whereas specific religions hold to confessional beliefs and doctrines that are "mere beliefs." Hick's "God" or the "Real" is just as much an assumption, "mere belief," as is the Christian's "Jesus Christ as the complete revelation of God." Actually, the Christian's position is superior in that it has at least some empirical grounding in the historical Jesus, whereas Hick's "God" or the "Real" is a totally abstract concept—a projection of his own philosophical imagination that can mean whatever he wishes to make it mean. It has a certain philosophical meaning for Hick, namely the modern Western enlightenment view of "God" which he projects as being the universal meaning for all persons, the "given" accepted or assumed by all persons. Hick calls for a new "Copernican revelation," to take Christianity out of the center of the world's religions and replace it with "God" or the "Real," which means his own philosophical concept of "reality."[7] Lesslie Newbigin points out that "The Hickian revolution is exactly the opposite of the Copernican. It is a move from a view centered in the objective reality of the man Jesus Christ, to a view centered in my own subjective conception of ultimate reality."[8] The arrogance of Hick as he supposedly attacks the arrogance of the "West" is painfully obvious. For a thorough critique of Hick's use of his own Western enlightenment philosophy as the ultimate criterion in the name of "world democracy" see "A Politics of Speech" by Kenneth Surin.[9] But however these facts may be, we need to look carefully at the reasons given for a theology based on religious relativism.

Those who advocate religious relativism as the starting point for doing theology, stress first the fact that religion because of absolutist claims has been one of the major sources of strife and warfare among peoples. That Christianity has not been the only religion to make such absolutists claims only underscores the truth of this observation. The tragic history of religious warfare is well known and needs no elaboration. Second, they stress that religion, particularly absolutist religion, has been used both as a rationale and as a tool for political, social, and economic conquest and oppression. The centuries-old institution of feudalism grounded to a large extent in religion, the religious support for slavery, the caste system in India, racial prejudice in Christendom, religious wars across history, and hundreds of other examples make clear the demonic nature of religion in many of its manifestations. Religion in one way or another has been an ally and component of most of the racial, ethnic, tribal, and national bigotry that has afflicted the globe. This is particularly true of so-called "established religions" where church and state are combined into one. One of the wisest provisions in the United States Constitution is that there shall be no establishment of religion. A good case could be made for the contention that religion has been one of the scourges of humankind.

No one would question that the divisive and oppressive factors of religion must be removed from the human scene. And in so far as these factors root in claims of one religion to be the true religion and therefore superior to all others, such superiority claims must be abandoned. A theology based on relativism, according to its proponents, would foster equality, would tend to eliminate superiority claims, and thus would aid in developing the religious life of humankind free of conflict. That this would not necessarily be the case is of course also true. Religion based on philosophical relativism can be just as oppressive as any other. It, too, can get some kind of "official sanction" and become oppressive.

Third, we all recognize that the explosive world in which we live with the threat of atomic holocaust hanging over us, adds to the urgency for unity and the removal of as many divisive factors from the human family as possible. A "world religion" creating harmony and binding people together around common beliefs and common values (the word religion comes from the Latin word meaning "bind together") is certainly a worthy goal. The need to remove every divisive factor possible from the human scene and to promote every unifying factor possible for the human race is not only desirable but imperative if we are to avoid a world catastrophe. But is relativism the way to achieve this goal? I do not think so. There is a much more effective way, as I will show later.

Fourth, in the modern world, where today across the globe the old oppressive political, social, economic, and religious forces are gradually giving way to democracy, the spirit of tolerance and respect for the culture, social customs, and religious beliefs and practices of others is imperative. That the various religious traditions have arisen out of cultural factors, some of which are peculiar to the particular cultures, and some of which are common to mankind, is simply a fact. Therefore, the relativity of the various religions to each other is simply an obvious fact that must be recognized. Respect for all cultures and all religions is mandatory. The dignity and the personhood of every person, regardless of race, gender, ethnic origin, nationality, or religion must be respected and honored. But this, as we will seek to show, in no sense requires religious relativism.

Fifth, the advocates of a relativistic "universal theology of religion" point out that the doctrines and beliefs of the Christian faith are interrelated with those of other religions both in terms of origin and development. Christianity is founded in Judaism, out of which it arises. Some have even spoken of Christianity as a "Jewish heresy." They point out that the teachings and sayings of Jesus have parallels in Judaism and in other religions. Likewise, Christianity was greatly influenced in its development by the Greek mystery cults and other religions and philosophies of the day. So they ask, "Where is the uniqueness?" And in terms of abstract ethical teachings they are right. Judaism, Buddhism, and other religions have many high ethical and moral teachings. This is the reason we stress *who* Jesus Christ *was* and is and *what* he embodied in his own person, not what he taught. He was God (including all of the moral and ethical teachings and principles) embodied in human flesh. This is his uniqueness. The uniqueness in the Christian faith is simply the Incarnation, that is, that Jesus was the "Word [God] become flesh" (John 1:14).

Likewise, we have to recognize that Christians (who are simply sinners saved by grace) have in the past and continue in the present to fall victims to sinful pride and arrogance, which gives them a sense of superiority over others. In ancient times the Jewish people clearly felt themselves superior to Gentiles. So Christians, in time mostly Gentiles, felt that they had to have a basis for feeling superior to Jews and others. In fact, the need to feel superior seems to be a basic human need growing out of our "fallen" state, that is, out of our sinful nature. Both Greeks and Romans felt themselves to be superior to "barbarians." Jews knew they were superior to "Gentiles." The Chinese spoke of China as the "central kingdom" and saw themselves as superior to all others. They spoke of the Europeans who showed up on their shores in the seventeenth and eighteenth centuries as "bearded barbarians." The empress of China, writing a letter to Queen Victoria, addressed her as "Chieftainess of the Tribe." Japanese considered themselves to be superior people of the rising sun, and from the end of the eighteenth century to near the end of the nineteenth century closed their country to all outsiders lest they be contaminated by other cultures. Certainly citizens of the United States of America feel superior—even calling ourselves "Americans" as though Canada, Central, and South America did not exist.

Even within the United States, the need to be "number one" is almost pathological. A book was written a few years ago titled *The Ugly American* which showed up our arrogant attitudes. Each year we play a "world series" in baseball that up until recently included only teams in the United States, and now only the United States and Canada. So, many argue, the claim to Christian uniqueness is nothing but ethnic and religious pride, and to our shame we must confess that Christians have been guilty of such sinful pride. The fact that this same ethnic and religious pride is also expressed in some of the other religions as superiority and exclusiveness does not alter the fact being pointed out here about Christians.

Thus, the theologians of religious relativism argue, we must, in the words of John Hick, quoted above, experience a new "Copernican revolution." Copernicus took the earth out of the center of the universe and placed it in orbit around the sun along with the other planets. In the same way, Christianity, according to Hick, must be taken out of the center as the one true religion and placed in orbit along with the other religions of the world. It must be viewed as one religion among many, each of which is historically based, having arisen out of its own culture. Each has unique aspects, and each is related to the others in the same way that most cultures are interrelated. There is no absolute culture, and there is no absolute religion. What can we say about all of this?

First, as regards the relativity of religions, I agree completely. What I want to stress in this entire essay is that we present a *person* and proclaim a *way*—not a religion. The world's religions are indeed relative to each other, and this seems obvious to anyone who looks at the facts. All religions have features—beliefs and practices—that appear from different vantage points to be either desirable or undesirable. This is as true of the so-called "higher" religions as of the so-called "primitive" religions. Thus, it seems obvious that there is no such thing as an absolute religion, Christianity included. Christianity is a religion like all other religions and is culturally conditioned. Across history some awful things have been done by Christians and even done in the name of Christianity. However, the recognition that Christianity is simply one religion among many does not in any way preclude the possibility that the object of Christian faith, Jesus Christ, may be unique and absolute. This question is left open. Likewise, as a matter of fact, the question as to whether the object of faith in any other religion, such as Mohammed, Buddha, Krishna, etc., is absolute, also remains open. I am speaking theoretically here, but it is important to make clear that dealing with this question of whether the object of faith in any given religion is absolute, is different from dealing with the question of whether a given religion is absolute. The latter asks whether a given empirical reality is absolute, whereas the former asks whether there can be an absolute in the reality of which we are all a part, the reality we speak of broadly as the universe.

Furthermore, if one is going to take the position that there is an absolute in the universe, he/she must give reasons for taking this position and must seek by whatever means possible to substantiate the claim. Recognizing that we are dealing with an area of life and a dimension of existence that does not lend itself readily to scientific testing and where the scientific approach is at best limited, we must nevertheless look at all the facts, all the evidence available, and thus arrive at that which squares best with the totality of reality. In other words, we will be honest and open and seek to arrive at that which, in view of all the facts we can ascertain, makes the most sense. That questions will remain is certain. Also, in final analysis, a "leap of faith" is inevitable. However, it should never be a blind leap of faith, but an informed, reasoned leap of faith. After a rigorous, reasoned, and open-minded search, a leap of faith to an absolute is not only justified and legitimate, as William James shows, but in the final analysis both necessary and inevitable. We all stand somewhere on some absolute (or absolutes) whether we recognize where we stand or not. In what follows I wish to make clear where I stand, that is, the absolute on which I stand. I will argue that all religions, including Christianity, are relative, but that the revelation in Jesus Christ is absolute.

THE CASE FOR A THEOLOGY BASED ON RELIGIOUS ABSOLUTES

This last statement that I hold Jesus Christ to be absolute demands that we ask another question: What do we mean when we say that Jesus Christ is absolute? This question of absolutes is one that needs to be clarified. Holding to absolutes is often equated with being arrogant or dogmatic. For example, Leonard Swidler in his book *After the Absolute*,[10] confuses holding absolutes with being dogmatic and bigoted ("Mine is the only true religion," etc). When he speaks about "after the absolute," what he is really talking about is "after dogmatism" and "after bigotry." Swidler is right that we must get rid of bigotry, but this is entirely different from getting rid of absolutes. This is a false identification. One may believe in and hold to absolutes without in any way being dogmatic or arrogant. The belief that Jesus Christ is the absolute and ultimate revelation of both God as he is, and humankind as created to be, is the absolute that I hold to. In fact, I reject outright the enlightenment, Deist position that there is a genus called "religion" and all specific religions are species of this genus. In terms of Kantian epistemology, this genus called "religion" is the noumena (Hick: "Real"; Samartha: "Mystery") of which specific religions are the phenomena. This view roots in the medieval philosophy of Realism in which Universals are seen as ultimately real. As will become clear in what follows, I reject this "Realism." There can be no real dialogue of religion when all of the religions of mankind are melted into the one philosophical concoction based on the Western enlightenment philosophy expressed by John Hick. It is my contention that only as each religion is true to its own essence, true to its own "absolutes," can there be any meaningful dialogue. Why dialogue when Hick and company have resolved all the differences, melted all of the religions down into one, and created a unitary pluralistic "universal theology of religion?" What is there to dialogue about? Only as I hold firmly to my absolute, Jesus Christ, and my neighbor holds to his or her absolute is meaningful dialogue possible.

In order to make clear the reason for this claim and to make clear what is meant by saying that Jesus Christ is absolute, and in general what is meant by the absolutist position as over against the relativist position in theology, we need to look at the essential nature of religion. The first thing we need to note is that every religious tradition, or religion, is a "worldview," whether articulated or simply implied. This is true whether the tradition is a world religion embracing millions, or a small tribal faith. A worldview may be said to be comprised of two basic components: (1) values and conduct systems and (2) beliefs and fact-claims about the universe in which we live. Both of these components are expressed in the many facets of the religious tradition: rituals, patterns of worship, beliefs, mores, customs, taboos, the self-understanding of the adherents, etc. Our question is, how do these components relate to the question of what is absolute in religion, if anything, and what is relative.

In regard to the first component, namely the value and conduct systems, it will be observed that the question of absoluteness as regards these systems *as* systems is irrelevant. Value and conduct systems in a given society, or religion, are simply what the people value and what they consider right and wrong. Such systems vary from one religion to another, and everyone recognizes that they are relative to each other. However, this fact has nothing to do with the question as to whether there are ethical standards or values which are absolute. Cultural relativity is a fact, but cultural relativity does not imply ethical relativity. Whether there is an absolute standard of "right" conduct or an absolute system of values by which the beliefs, mores, and values of a given religion can be tested, moves us over into the second component, namely the area of beliefs and "fact-claims" about reality, or about the universe in which we live.

Turning to this second component, we find that in contrast to the first, the question of absoluteness, of truth or falsity is quite relevant. In this component the adherents of the religion believe that their worldview, both in its empirical and in its nonempirical aspects, is a true and correct reading of reality. The claim, whether expressed or unexpressed, is that reality is as they perceive it, including the object of their faith and commitment. In regard to the empirical claims that may be involved, an empirical test can be devised to determine if the claims are true or false. For example, ancient religions and other worldviews believed the world to be flat. Empirical testing has shown this belief about reality to be false.

On the other hand, the nonempirical claims of a religion cannot be so tested. For example, it is not possible to prove that either the claim held by Jews, Muslims, and Christians that "There is a God," or the claim held by Buddhists that "There is no God" is true or false. Such claims can neither be verified nor falsified in the sense of empirical proof that would compel the reasonable skeptic to say, "The existence of God has now been proven," or for the believer to say, "I now accept the fact that the existence of God has been disproven." In regard to the belief in a flat earth, such proof is clearly possible, but not in regard to the existence of God.

Does this mean, then, that the question of the truth or falsity of nonempirical "fact-claims" is irrelevant? Not at all. If a fact-claim is not verifiable at present, but is verifiable in principle at some future time, then linguistically the claim has "meaning" and the question of the truth or falsity of the claim is a valid question whether the claim is empirical or nonempirical. For example the empirical claim that there are human beings on Mars is either true or false, though not verifiable at present. If and when we ever arrive on Mars, the claim can be shown to be either true or false. Or, as pointed out by Lesslie Newbigin,[11] for a long time Einstein affirmed the truth of his theory of relativity, but could not at the time prove it scientifically. It was only years later that technical applications of the theory proved the theory valid. It was true all along, but could not be called a "truth" until proven valid.

Exactly the same is true with the nonempirical fact-claim that there is conscious existence after death. This claim cannot be verified at present However, it will be proven to be either true or false for each person after death. If there is no conscious life after death, then the claim will have been falsified, though obviously the person dying will not be aware of its being falsified, and those still on earth will not know that the claim has been falsified. However, if there is conscious life after death, the claim will have been verified and the person passing through death will be aware that the claim is verified, though persons still on earth will not know this and will have to await their own death in order to find out. Thus the question of the truth or falsity of the nonempirical fact-claim that there is conscious life after death is a valid and important question. John Hick sets this kind of verification forth in his parable of the "celestial city," and speaks of it as "eschatological verification."[12]

We should note however, that though the claims that there is a God or that there is conscious existence after death may actually be true and may be so verified eschatologically, it is not legitimate to speak of them—or of any other nonempirical fact-claims of religion—as "truths." Calling various nonempirical fact-claims "truths" or "religious truths" is, in my judgment, a common error made by theologians and other religious writers. These claims or beliefs have not been, and cannot be, proven in this life, and in fact may actually turn out to be false when verified eschatologically. So the word truth is not appropriate. To use the word truth for a cherished belief, no matter how strongly held and widely accepted, is to dilute and weaken the force of the word truth. William Zuurdeeg calls the human being "homo convictus,"[13] who holds to beliefs (convictions) passionately and wishes to convict others. In the effort to do so, he/she may be guilty of what I call a theological or philosophical version of "pounding the pulpit." "Truth" sounds much stronger than "belief" or "claim"; so our "beliefs" become "truths."[14] We will examine the use of the words true and truth in more detail in the next chapter, and the reasons for my insistence that we not speak of beliefs as "truths" will become clearer.

We are now in position to discuss relativism as over against absolutism in religion, and to look in more detail at my claim that Jesus Christ is the absolute. The proponents of a pluralistic or relativistic theology insist that everything in religion is relative. There are no absolutes. What can we say about this claim? We have noted that both the value systems and the conduct systems actually held by the different religious communities are indeed relative to each other. Also we have noted that the empirical fact-claims in a religion are verifiable, at least in principle, and any claims in this regard are simply either true or false. The nonempirical fact-claims are only verifiable eschatologically, which means that this side of the grave we cannot know with scientific certainty whether they are true or false. There is no way to know with scientific certainty this side of the grave whether the theism of the Judeo-Christian/Islamic worldview or the non-theism of the Buddhist worldview is in accord with reality—that is, which of these two fact-claims is true, if either is.

Now the question arises: Since all the nonempirical fact-claims of the various worldviews or religions are unproven and unprovable empirically, are they not simply "beliefs"? The answer is "yes." However, this fact that we cannot have scientific certainty in regard to these nonempirical fact-claims does not in any way imply that there are no absolutes. In fact, we all of necessity stand on some absolute, even if our absolute is that there are no absolutes (a contradiction in terms), else there is only complete skepticism or agnosticism, and we can make no assertion whatever. Also we need to be aware that our absolutes, our ultimate presuppositions are always "faith" positions. They cannot be otherwise since empirical proof is impossible in regard to these ultimates. Absolutes in this sense are beliefs about the nature of reality and are a powerful force in human life. Such beliefs also imply of necessity that contradictory beliefs are false. In other words, we all of necessity hold to or assume certain absolutes. But, as we have argued above, the belief that there are absolutes is no more of a faith position than the belief that all is relative. Relativism is certainly no more proven than is absolutism. Each position— (1) that all is relative or (2) that all is not relative but that there are certain absolutes—stands on exactly the same footing as a "faith assumption" or a "starting point." We all stand somewhere, whether or not we are consciously or deliberately aware of where we stand.

Conscious self-understanding or awareness of where we stand has many facets. My own self-understanding involves the belief that Jesus Christ is God. Jesus Christ was God incarnate for thirty-three years and as the risen Lord is today the second person of the Trinity, God the Father, Son, and Holy Spirit. Jesus Christ is in the Christian understanding of the Trinity, "God the Son" or "God the Redeemer." This is one of my absolutes, my most fundamental absolute. It is a nonconfirmed fact-claim about reality. That is, it is nonconfirmed scientifically, though I would like to qualify this statement somewhat by pointing out that there is a kind of scientific verification possible as suggested early in this century by E. Stanley Jones and others. It is the method of testing by rigorously putting beliefs into the burning crucible of daily living or what might be called, "experiential testing." This type of testing is valid, but is limited in that it unavoidably involves a certain amount of subjectivity, which makes possible differences in the interpretation of results.

I am willing to dialogue in reference to this belief. In fact, this is the only way that we can dialogue and relate to each other in honesty. I clearly recognize that my belief, my absolute, may be wrong. I certainly respect and am happy to listen to those who hold to contradictory absolutes, as for example, the atheist. But this is the absolute on which I stand and on which I stake my life. Furthermore, it is not a blind or arbitrary absolute. I am aware that one may hold to an absolute on arbitrary and insufficient grounds, as for example the belief that the earth is flat. But such need not be the case. Indeed, I have put my absolute to every test, both intellectual and experiential, that I know of, particularly to the test of living. It remains my absolute because I always find it confirmed by life. It is no theoretical or "armchair" absolute but one that grows out of the struggle with the issues of life. I find that Jesus Christ is the revelation of the way life is made to work. His way squares with reality as I experience it. So whether we come from revelation down or from science and the facts of life up, we arrive at the same place. It is in this sense that I claim Jesus Christ as the absolute on which I build both my theology and my life, the unique revelation of God and thus a revelation of the way we all are made to live.

I make no claim for Christianity. It is relative to all other religions, historically, culturally, and in every way. My only absolute is Jesus Christ, the Word (God) become flesh. In fact, I would not go around the corner to introduce you to Christianity. But I would go around the world to introduce you to Jesus Christ. This claim concerning Jesus Christ is of course a faith-claim, as are all absolutes, and raises a number of questions that relate to New Testament studies and to what we really know about Jesus Christ from a historical perspective. This question has had exhaustive study, and many books have been written on the subject. To attempt to go into this extensive research would take us far afield from the purpose of this essay. But we hope in what follows to make clear why we hold Jesus

Christ to be the absolute revelation of God. It is my firm conviction, increasingly supported by New Testament scholars such as Gunther Bornkamm and Luke Johnson, and by theologians such as Wolfhart Pannenberg and others, that though there remain many questions about the historical Jesus, we can know enough about him to know who he was and is, and, more importantly, because he is risen, living today as a person, we can know him in person in existential I–Thou encounter.

Likewise, we can test his way against what works in the world and what does not work. Our claim that he is the Way can be tested in daily living. And, in fact, we are actually doing it all the time, whether we realize it or not. The famous "Moral Re-armament Movement" in Great Britain spoken of as the "Oxford Movement" subscribed to four absolutes: absolute honesty, absolute purity, absolute unselfishness, and absolute love. They were under no illusion that they could be perfect, but they set these absolutes as a goal toward which to strive and against which to measure themselves. A skeptical British army officer in India was talking with the late Dr. E. Stanley Jones about this movement. Both cynically and in jest he said, "I'm going to start my movement and call it the 'Cambridge Movement.' I will have four absolutes also." Historically Oxford University and Cambridge University have been rivals and competitors, on opposite sides of issues. The army officer, making a play on this rivalry, said, "My absolutes will be absolute dishonesty, absolute impurity, absolute selfishness, and absolute hate." He said it as a kind of joke, but Stanley Jones replied: "That's a good idea. Why don't you try it?" The officer thought for a moment and then said, "Well actually I guess I couldn't. It would not work. I would be knocked off before noon." And he would. Absolute hate, absolute dishonesty simply would not work. Absolute hate would mean killing every person you met. How long would one last doing this? Would absolute dishonesty, absolute impurity, absolute selfishness, absolute hate work in society? The clear answer is: absolutely not. Society would fall apart. It is not the way. It is contrary to the Way God has made human beings and human society to work. It is the exact opposite of the Way of Christ.

Would absolute honesty, absolute love, absolute unselfishness, absolute purity work? They would work beautifully. Economic, political, social, and international relationships would hum like a new, well-oiled electric motor. Peace and justice would bring joy and well-being to all. Just as an automobile runs on gasoline and not on water because this is the way the automobile is made to run, so society would work beautifully on the Way of Jesus Christ because this is the way God has made society to work. This seems like fairly good scientific proof that Jesus Christ is the Way—the way that works! It is reported that when President Wilson of the United States, Lord George of Great Britain, and Clemenceau of France sat down at the Versailles Palace in 1918 to draw up the peace treaty that closed World War I, Wilson was urging mercy and forgiveness toward the Germans. At one point it is reported that Clemenceau sneered: "Mr. Wilson, you talk like Jesus Christ!" Wilson's admonitions were rejected. Vengeance was written into the treaty. The result within ten years was the rise of Hitler, the Third Reich, the holocaust, and the carnage of World War II.

When a peace treaty was drawn up between the United States and Japan at the close of World War II, the opposite approach was followed. It was decided to forgive the attack at Pearl Harbor and to help Japan get back on its feet. Now for over fifty years, peace and cooperation have continued to the benefit of all. Is this the way that works? It seems to me that the evidence is crystal clear: Jesus Christ is the Way, the only way that ultimately will work. And this is absolute!

Having stated the absolute to which I hold, the question immediately arises, does holding to the view that Jesus Christ is the absolute revelation both of God as he is and of human life as it was made to be lived, of necessity make the Christian arrogant and bigoted? This is a good question, and for many, as witnessed in hundreds of writings, the answer is "Yes." But let us examine this claim that believing in absolutes and particularly that Jesus Christ is absolute, of necessity makes one arrogant and bigoted.

We have stated that we recognize the relativity of religions as parts of the cultures in which they have arisen and in which they have developed. Nevertheless, it is clear that religions, however they have developed, do have beliefs which either make or imply fact-claims about reality and these fact-claims are either true or false. Therefore, every worldview or religion has certain absolutes. Taoism does not say "maybe there is the Tao." It says that ultimate reality, the order of the universe, is Tao. Belief in the Tao is absolute. Whether Taoists are right or wrong is another question. Likewise with the Hindu, Buddhist, Christian, or any other religious worldview.

So the question of arrogance, dogmatism, or a superiority complex comes not in holding to an absolute, but in how one relates to persons holding to other absolutes, even contrary absolutes. Is the person open to other views, willing to think and let think, show respect for those holding opposite opinions, willing to dialogue? Or does the person consign to oblivion those who do not hold to his or her absolute? I see no reason why I cannot hold firmly to my belief in the Christian doctrine of Incarnation (and when eschatological verification comes, I just may be right), without arrogance or a superiority complex. I am making no claim about myself or my religion, but about a person who not only lived two thousand years ago, but, who, according to my belief—my absolute—also is risen in person and lives today in person. I certainly respect those who disagree. I may be wrong. Being a Christian in no way makes me infallible or my religion superior or even better than any other. I am certainly open to other world-views and to other absolutes. I may be wrong, and those holding other worldviews may be right. All I can do, however, is to state what I firmly believe to be the nature of reality. How can I do otherwise? How can I force myself to believe what I really do not believe? Or how can I force myself to unbelieve what I really believe? Whether we come from revela-tion down or from science up, it is my personal experience that we come out with one answer: the Way of Jesus Christ is reality. This, for me, is confirmation that my absolute, my belief, is true, though as stated above, it remains a belief, not a truth. And so I hold firmly to my absolute, while remaining open to those who hold to other absolutes.

It should be pointed out further that our beliefs about reality, our worldviews, our absolutes, are not ordinarily something we arbitrarily choose. There are two sources of one's worldview at any given time: (1) the society into which one is born and (2) one's contacts with other world-views through reading, personal experiences, study, dialogue, etc. Exposing oneself to the world's great philosophies and religious traditions may alter one's worldview and in this sense, one may consciously choose his world-view. However, beliefs are only really changed by convincing evidence or cogent arguments, not by one being forced to change, or by forcing oneself to change in order to accommodate someone else, or to remove barriers to fellowship. When Galileo was forced by the church to recant his view that the earth moves around the sun, it is reported that he muttered under his breath, "But it does move." One cannot force oneself to unbelieve something that in his or her experience she or he is convinced is true. In my own personal experience I find that the Way of Jesus Christ is the way to live, that it is in harmony with reality, that when I live his way I live well, whereas when I live any other way I do not live well. Thus I cannot unbe-lieve what I know in personal experience to be true, namely that in Jesus Christ, reality (God) is revealed. This is the absolute on which I stand.

Again, I am open to other worldviews. That is, I am as open as I can be, recognizing who I am and what my commitments are. If I am truly open, I must be open to my own commitments and biases. The so-called "objective" view claimed by certain philosophers and scientists is pure fiction. We all start with certain presuppositions, which define who we are, including our own "biases," and we should openly recognize this. It is my view that we should gladly recognize and honor all religious traditions, study them and learn from them. All empirical religions are indeed relative, including Christianity, and we can be enriched by each. I will happily reason together (dialogue) with persons of other worldviews who hold to other absolutes. I will reason, witness to my convictions, and will expect my partner in dialogue to do the same. In fact, it is only on this basis that dialogue can be genuine and authentic. Those insisting on a pluralistic theology as a basis for dialogue are actually in danger of becoming the new imperialists. Their demand that Christians give up their absolutes in order to dialogue means that adherents of other religions must do the same. In other words, the pluralists are calling the shots: Everyone conform to our theology and then we can dialogue. Does not the proposal I am making here, namely that all hold to their absolutes in brotherly love, and dialogue about life in terms of these absolutes, point to a much more open quest and provide what is in fact the nonimperialistic way?

Indeed, this approach would seem to be the only way for honest dialogue to take place. Obviously we must start with creating friendships and with sharing our lives together, which we do every week in our local Ministerial Union with clergy and laity of all the various religions in our city. On the other hand, if we simply meet on terms set forth by the pluralistic theologians, all we do is talk about the supposed common denominators based on western enlightenment philosophy and never get to the inherently clashing worldviews of the particular religious traditions. I will happily dialogue on the basis of the real essence of the different traditions ("the real thing"), though I will not argue, for argument has no place in dialogue. Should I be convinced by another, I will change. But until I am convinced, in the words of Martin Luther, "Here I stand; I cannot do otherwise; so help me God." I certainly expect my partner in dialogue to do the same. I expect my partner to have absolutes, for sharing beliefs and their consequences in life is the heart of dialogue. In other words, I believe that we can hold firmly to religious absolutes in the midst of an age of religious pluralism. I can hold firmly to my belief that Jesus Christ is the absolute revelation both of God as he is and of human existence as it was created to be, and at the same time respect and honor other religions. In fact, the very essence of my Christian faith, as it focuses on the value of every person and on the call to respect and honor every person, demands it. I can witness to this faith and proclaim this message vigorously in an age of religious pluralism without arrogance. And if I do it in love and humility, as a Christian should, and in a way that respects the beliefs and the person-hood of all persons, also as a Christian should, I will be a proper witness to Christ and to the world mission of Christ to which I am commissioned. The world mission of the Christian church is as valid as ever, and I will seek to establish this claim further as we proceed.

Chapter Two
OFFER THEM CHRIST

THE TRUTH

CHAPTER ONE HAS DEALT WITH THE QUESTION OF ABSOLUTES AND of whether the world mission of the Christian church is still valid in the face of increasing religious pluralism and relativism. We have taken the position that Christianity as a religion is far from absolute, but that Jesus Christ, the divine–human person, God Incarnate, is absolute. He is the Way, spelled with a capital "W," and the Christian mission introducing and presenting Christ to all the world is as valid as it ever was. We have sought to defend this position in a provisional way, and will develop the argument further as we proceed. Presenting Jesus as the Absolute, however, immediately raises the question of truth. If Jesus Christ is absolute, then is not the religion founded by him the true and correct religion? Does not this implication open the door to the arrogant exclusivistic claims for Christianity as the only true religion, which were dominant prior to the twentieth century and which we reject? We need to take a careful and reasoned look at this matter of what is (or would be) a "true religion."

The first thing to note is that there is always a human element in any religion. No religion is simply handed down from heaven in complete form. A religion may have a divine source and a divine element in it, but it also always has a human element. It is always involved in and related to the culture in which it grows up and exists. There is a "people" element in every religion. Thus, no religion is absolute or simply "the true religion." As long as there are human elements, and there always are, no religion can be perfect.

The second factor involved is our understanding and use of the words "true" and "truth." Few words in the English language are more ambiguous and more confusing than these words. C. F. J. Williams says, "What sort of a thing is truth, and what sort of things are truths? Philosophers have found these questions very perplexing."[1] William Beardslee calls truth a "worn-out word."[2] And indeed in many ways it is. Leslie Armour points out that "There is no agreement—at least among philosophers—about how the concept of truth is to be construed" and that the "theories of truth which have been popular in the last hundred years—correspondence, coherence, and pragmatic theories—are so unlike one another as to raise the suspicion that they must be directed to the solution of different problems."[3] This uncertain meaning of truth makes one wary of using the term at all. An ambiguous word may cover a multitude of fuzzy thinking. Nevertheless, truth is an extremely important word. Our purpose in dealing with it here is to try to bring some clarification to its use in religious discourse, especially as this discourse is involved in the kind of dialogue that religious pluralism calls for.

In religious discourse one finds truth used in three basic ways, though there are a number of variations. First, there is the epistemological usage in which truth is used in the ordinary sense of the true–false dichotomy, and in this usage it means a statement, claim, belief, etc., which is not false. A synonym for true used in this sense is "correct." I will not enter into the subtleties of what it would mean to say that a claim is true as this issue would be debated by advocates of the various traditional correspondence, coherence, and pragmatic theories of truth. I simply refer to those claims which obviously are not false.

Second, there is the ontological usage in which truth is used as a synonym for reality. It is seen as a kind of entity in itself and corresponds to the use of *true* in which the term is a synonym for "genuine" or "real," as in such expressions as "true-blue," or "true gold,"or "true friend." Someone says, "We seek truth wherever it may be found" (the academic quest). Mahatma Gandhi said, "My God is Absolute Truth." *Truth* thus is seen as a kind of "something" to be sought or found. It is in this ontological sense that Williams asks, "What sort of a thing is truth?"

Third, there is the existential usage in which truth is seen as a quality of life, an existential encounter with the transcendent or with ultimate reality as in Emil Brunner's book, *Truth As Encounter*.[4] Kierkegaard speaks of this as "subjective" truth as over against "objective" truth. An example of this would be to say that a person's character or his religion is true. Another example would be when the word truth is used as a claim about values. Such truth of course involves opinions and preferences and is, at least to some extent, subjective.

We will initially pass over the first usage listed above, namely the epistemological, as I wish to base my proposal on it at the end of the chapter, and turn to the second usage listed, namely the ontological theory of truth. I will argue that the use of truth as an ontological category is unsound and that it confuses communication. The ontological usage has a long and honored history going back at least to Plato's "the good, the true, and the beautiful." One of the most recent expressions of it is Elliott Deutsch's, *On Truth: An Ontological Theory*[5] which we will discuss below. One hesitates to challenge this time-honored use of the term. But we must if we are to bring some degree of clarity into the task of interreligious discourse, a task which is quite crucial at the present stage in history.

ONTOLOGICAL USAGE

Ontological Usage Confusing

The ontological use of the word *truth* seems to confuse three things: (1) the definition or theory of truth; (2) the criterion of truth; and (3) the reality about which a truth-claim is made. Serious problems inhere in this confusion. Aristotle said, "To say of what is that it is, of what is not that it is not, is true." If *true* and *truth* were always used with this simple meaning of "a claim that is not false," then the matter would be quite simple: (1) the definition would be, "that claim which is not false"; (2) the criterion would be, "check the claim against the reality"; (3) the reality would be, not the truth but rather "that about which the truth-claim is made."

But when we begin to use truth to refer to the reality itself in an ontological sense, and not to the claim about that reality, we open the door to ambiguity and confusion. Leslie Armour points out concerning this ontological usage, "If truth is a component of the world, then, presumably, we must not only know the truth about the world, but the 'truth about the truth' as well, since the 'world' has as one of its components 'the truth' and the complete truth will thus contain the truth about that as well."[6] What is the meaning of the second *truth* in the phrase "the truth about the truth?" Stanley Samartha refers to the Hindu "Satyasya Satyam," which he translates as "the Truth of the Truth." He claims that this expression has some deep hidden meaning. I certainly would not question that there may be some subtle hidden meaning here, but would not a simple use of *truth* as the opposite of false, for the first truth in this phrase, and the word *reality* for the second truth in the phrase be clearer? We want to communicate— not speak in riddles. "The truth about reality" would seem much clearer.

The considerable confusion which has developed in our use of the words *true* and *truth* is well expressed by Alan White. He points out that "The things that we call 'true' fall into two classes, namely what is said and things other than what is said." He adds, "What is said includes what is said in statements, stories, accounts and remarks, and in expressions of beliefs, opinions, theories, etc."[7] The word when applied to things other than what is said takes the form of describing such realities as diamonds, colors, courage, friends, etc. Let us now examine this ontological usage further.

Ontological Usage Contrasted with Epistemological Usage

White shows that the word *true* is used in regard to each of these two classes—what is said (epistemological usage), and things other than what is said (ontological usage)—in radically different ways: Let me quote him somewhat at length:

> First and most important, we can inquire about the truth (or falsity) of a true statement or a true story, but not of a true Corgi or true courage.

> Second, a statement or a story, but not a Corgi or courage can be perfectly, entirely or only half true.

> Third, the discovery that something is not a true statement or a true story need throw not the slightest doubt on its status as a statement or story, whereas the discovery that something is not a true Corgi or does not display true courage does throw some doubt on its status as a Corgi or as courageous.

> Fourth, if what is said gives an account of my holiday, then if it is true, it gives a true account of my holiday; but if a Corgi is a companion, it does not follow that, if my dog is a true Corgi, it is a true companion.

Fifth, the use of "true" about what is said is both attributive and predicative, that is, we can say both "This is a true statement (or story)" and "This statement (or story) is true." With things other than what is said, "true" can be used only attributively. We can say "This is a true Corgi (or true courage)" but not "This Corgi (or courage) is true." A true statement or story is a statement or story which is true, just as a long and involved statement or story is a statement or story which is long and involved. But although an admirable Corgi is a Corgi which is admirable and rare courage is courage which is rare, a true Corgi is not a Corgi which is true.

Sixth, "true" and "false" are proper equivalents only of what is said. If X is not a true statement, it is a false statement; and vice-versa. But to say that X is not a true Corgi is not to say that it is a false Corgi, nor is to say that these are false teeth necessarily to say that they are not true teeth any more than to say that X is not real cream is to say that it is unreal cream or to say that something has an unreal air about it is to say that it is not a real air. [8]

When the usage of a word has become this confused, is there any hope that it will ever have a clear and distinct meaning? This question of meaning is the most perplexing problem with regard to the ontological usage of truth. If a reader of religious literature will pause every time the word *truth* appears and ask, "What precisely does the writer mean by the word, or to what precisely does the writer refer?" he may find himself chasing the end of a rainbow. Often the writer uses the term as though he is quite certain that he has a real something in mind, but closer examination reveals that no such "entity" or "something" is clearly in mind at all. One can raise the question as to whether truth is used with any clear meaning at all unless the question "truth about what?" is appropriate and answerable.

Ontological Usage Linguistically Flawed

I am raising, of course, the linguistic question of meaning. Does truth in the sense of an entity in and of itself, have any linguistic meaning? "A truth" as the noun for a statement or claim or belief which is not false, has meaning, but truth as a term for an entity in and of itself is meaningless.

Despite the common idiom, does "true gold" really mean anything more than "gold?" Does not a claim that it is true gold simply mean that one believes it is actually gold? If it is in fact gold, it is gold, not true gold. If it is not "true gold" in the sense intended by the phrase, then it simply is not gold; it may be an alloy or a totally different substance; so adding the word true is meaningless. Now if one means pure or unalloyed gold, then this should be said, for it is quite correct that something could be gold and yet not be 100 percent gold. This same reasoning which is applicable to the attributive usage could be applied to any use of true or truth in the substantive sense. There is certainly nothing inherently wrong in speaking of pure gold as "true gold," for this is a common idiom, but the ambiguous use of true does create a problem for discussions in general. In addition, in every case of such usage there seems to be a better, more descriptive, more accurate term such as genuine or 100 percent, or "unalloyed," or "real," or simply the thing itself without a modifying adjective.

That the use of the words true and truth in this substantive and attributive sense has become idiomatic is quite clear, and I do not wish to nitpick idioms. The reason I am raising the issue is because the usage creates a problem which, in serious interreligious relationships, causes considerable difficulties. If "truth" or "religious truth" is an ontological "something," then is it the same for all religions? Or does it differ from religion to religion? Can something be a "truth" in one religion and not in another? If so, how is the word *truth* being used? Is it not simply a synonym for "belief?" For a genuine "truth" is true (if the word means what it is generally understood to mean) wherever it is found. There is a hopeless confusion in the use of language here.

Deutsch says, "This then, is the meaning of truth in religious language: the language is true when it fulfills its intentionality; when it is what it ought to be as revelator; as directive of self to reality; as formative of consciousness in relation to reality." In other words, the test of truth here is, "Does the language work?" Any language that achieves its purpose is true, and, in this sense, Nazi language that achieves its purpose is as true as Biblical or Qur'anic language that achieves its purpose. In regard to criterion Deutsch says:

> The test for truth in religious language involves the determination by someone (who, on the basis of his own experience and sensitivity, is qualified to make the determination) that the given

religious language is right for itself and is thus, not contradicted
by experience. [9]

The implication is that religious discourse is composed of "language
games" or what R. M. Hare calls "Bliks." Anyone—Jim Jones, Elijah D.
Mohammed, or the Pope—could determine what truth is. Truth as
commonly understood in the sense of *veritas* or that which is verified, has
no place. The ontological usage of *truth* in religious discourse therefore
breaks down.

EXISTENTIAL USAGE

I turn now to the existential usage of *truth*. Kierkegaard uses truth in the
sense of what he calls "subjective truth." Such "subjective truth" as distin-
guished from "objective truth," refers to one's inner integrity of life. It is
being true to one's inner essence. It is "living truthfully." While it is possible,
as Alice in *Alice in Wonderland* says, that we can make words mean what we
want them to mean, it is also important that in speaking and in writing we
communicate meaning. This is particularly the case in interreligious
discourse. The ambiguous use of a term impedes clarity and often leads to
the anomaly that the participants think there has been communication when
there has not been. The use of true and truth in the existential sense in my
judgment impedes communication and confuses dialogue because true and
truth clearly carry the connotation of "true–false" and one's inner life simply
is. If we are going to speak of it as "true," we must make clear the answer to
the question, "true to what?" There must be an agreed criterion.

Wilfred Cantwell Smith's Approach
One of the foremost proponents of existential usage of truth is Wilfred
Cantwell Smith, Harvard professor and author in the area of world religions. His book, *Questions of Religious Truth*,[10] deals extensively with the
question of truth in religion, holding that truth inheres in persons, not in
the religion. He rejects the ontological theory, stating that religions as such
are neither true nor false. He raises the question:

> You may say that the religious life of a given tribe is beautiful
> or ugly, edifying or wicked, rational or grotesque, poetic or
> prosaic, helpful or obstructive, cohesive or disruptive; you may

say that it is the opiate of the people, or the form of social
progress, the channel through which they know God insofar as
they do know Him, or a totally human contrivance with no
relevance to the divine; you may say that it is pleasing to God,
or displeasing. But what would you mean by saying that it is
true or false?[11]

Smith's point is well made and obviously correct. A careful student of
the religious traditions of humankind, Smith opts for the term "religious
tradition" rather than "religion" which he holds to be an inaccurate
"western" term. He points out that:

The religious traditions of mankind are facts, not theories. . . .
They are simply there, like Mount Everest. Like Mount Everest,
you may like them, or you may not . . . Yet, whatever your attitude to them, they are more like Mount Everest than they are
like a proposition in science. The latter may be true or false, but
historical facts and social institutions are existent actualities.[12]

What Smith states here seems to be obvious. In rejecting the ontological theory of truth, I have also ruled out a "true religion." However,
Smith is nevertheless deeply concerned about truth in religion. Our only
quarrel with Smith is in regard to his definition of truth and where he
seeks to locate truth. He seems to overlook the fact that whereas it is
quite true that religions as such are simply existent realities, neither true
nor false, these religions do make claims about reality and these claims
are either true or false. As to the importance of truth in religion, Smith
says, "Religious truth is utterly crucial; it is the paramount and
inescapable issue, before which all other religious matters, however
mighty, must bow."[13]

After making such a strong affirmation of the crucial importance of
truth, however, Smith bases his answer to the question of religious truth,
insofar as he is actually dealing with truth and not with something else, on
a logical fallacy, the fallacy of ambiguity. "Are religions true or false?"
Smith asks. His answer is that the truth or falsity is in the persons who
adhere to the faith, not in the beliefs or claims of the religion itself. What
Smith avers is extremely important, but it does not answer the question
which he has asked. When he says, "I have urged the personalist quality of

religious life as of ultimate significance over against abstract systems,"[14] I could not agree more. But this is not the issue at hand. It does not answer the question he has asked.

An illustration may help. Two botanists are discussing the effect of a certain insect on the orange. They are aware that the issue is controversial because though the insect is definitely harmful, there are some beneficial side effects. They take opposite positions, one arguing that the net effect of the insect is harmful and the other that the net effect is beneficial. In the midst of the argument a third party walks up, and perceiving what is going on, immediately "solves" the issue. He points out that there is no real problem, for after all orange is a color and the insect has no effect one way or the other on color.

This shift in meaning is precisely what Smith has done. The question of whether I live my religion is a crucial one assuming that my religion has high standards and ideals—or even if it has demeaning ones, it is still crucial. I can certainly be true to my religious faith—that is, exemplify its precepts in my life. Or I may be false to it. But my faithfulness to my religious precepts says nothing about whether the precepts are true or good. Witness the Jim Jones cult. I agree completely with Smith that religions are neither true nor false. They simply are. But the question as to whether the claims which a religion makes or implies (its beliefs, doctrines, presuppositions) are true, is a legitimate question. And this question is not answered by the way in which Smith turns it into a totally different kind of question. To state that the truth or falsity resides in the adherents, how faithfully they live their beliefs, says nothing about whether the beliefs are themselves true or false. And what is more, it raises serious questions about the use of the words *true* and *truth*. One may be as true to his Nazi religion as another is to his Christian faith. But the faithfulness of neither says anything about the truth or falsity of the beliefs or claims of either religion.

Truth of Religion Different from Living True to One's Religion

In regard to Islam, Smith says, "It matters less whether Islam as an impersonal and ineffective entity, in essence but not in existence, is true or not—and indeed, it means less—than whether the actual Islam of Muslim X and Muslim Y and Muslim Z is true religion or how far it is."[15] Smith surely cannot mean this. He obviously assumes that the precepts of Islam are worthy precepts, and are not Nazi or demonic precepts. The question of the nature of Islam is crucial and cannot be so easily side-stepped. The fallacy of Smith's statement becomes apparent if we substitute "Nazism" for "Islam" and "Nazi" for "Muslim." The content of one's religion is important, not just whether he lives the religion. Indeed to live a demonic religion is worse than professing it and not living it.

Smith is right when he says, "To say that Christianity is true does not tell us anything about how false the Christianity of Mr. Q may have been last week when he was putting across some real estate deal."[16] However, the reverse is also true. To say that the Christianity of Mr. Q is true does not tell us anything about whether the basic beliefs of Christianity are true. Smith's concern is for a high-quality lived religion, and we admire his passion for "religion that is pure and undefiled" (James 1:27). But we have to confess that we do not think he really means what he says. To say that how well one lives his religion is more important than "any question of the truth or otherwise of 'his religion' in the abstract, formal, systematic sense of the religion of his historical community generally"[17] is to affirm that there is no basic difference in the Quakers and the Jim Jones cult, or between the Church of England and Nazism. Smith, of course, does not intend this. His enthusiasm for a "lived religion" has carried him too far. He obviously has some hidden presuppositions about the truth of the beliefs and teachings of Christianity. In other words, Smith sidesteps the question of the truth of Christianity as a religion, while at the same time presupposing that the beliefs of Christianity are "true" as over against those of Nazism. What Smith is talking about is something quite different from the question of the truth-claims of Christianity or Islam as over against the truth-claims of some other system or ideology, but he nevertheless presupposes this truth. For if just living a religion makes it true, then Hitler certainly made Nazism true.

Can Religions "Become True"?

Smith's understanding of religious truth as the question of whether I live my religion enables him to talk about a religion "becoming true": "Even those who like to think that religions have been false in the past should hope that they will become true in the future."[18]

He says, "Christianity, I suggest, is not true absolutely, impersonally, statistically; rather it can become true, if and as you or I appropriate it to our lives and interiorize it, insofar as we live it out from day to day. It becomes true as we take it off the shelf and personalize it in dynamic actual existence."[19] Smith even speaks of the Qur'an as "becoming true." He says,

> Might we say that the statement "the Qur'an is the word of God" rather than being in itself true or false . . . can become true—in the life of a particular person; and further, that it has become true in the lives of many persons; and further, that it has become more true in the lives of certain persons at certain times, than others?[20]

What does "become true" mean? The Qur'an either is the word of God or it is not. Therefore, the statement, "The Qur'an is the word of God" is either true or it is false. What would it mean for the statement "The Qur'an is the word of God" to become true? The statement, "It is raining" could be false (if it is not raining) and then become true if it started raining. In this case the circumstances described by the claim changed. In this sense a statement can become true.[21] But such is not the case with the Qur'an. The Qur'an has been what it is for centuries. It does not change. Therefore, unless the circumstances change—which in this case would have to be a change in God or in what it meant to be the "word of God"—how could the statement "The Qur'an is the word of God" at one time be untrue and later become true? To say that the statement "The Qur'an is the word of God" becomes operative in the person or becomes a force in the person's life, or becomes alive and real for the person, makes sense. But to say that the Qur'an "becomes true" does not.

Can We Know if Religions Are True or False?

Smith's treatment of religious truth seems to cause confusion in his own mind as to whether it is possible to know the truth of religion. After vigorously arguing that religious truth is in persons, not in the traditions themselves, he speaks of religious traditions "that do not hold the view that final religious truth has been given in the past."[22] In this statement Smith assumes that truth is in the tradition itself. Further, he says:

> I have no hesitation in putting forward that no man in one life-time of study could possibly become sufficiently well informed on the history of either the Buddhist or the Hindu communities

> to be able to say that Buddhism or Hinduism is true or alternately
> is false, and know what he was saying.[23]

This statement again assumes that the truth, which cannot be discovered, is nevertheless in the religion itself and not, as Smith claims elsewhere, in the adherents. Smith needs to make up his mind. Howard Burkle in a critique of Hendrik Kraemer asks, "How can any human being know enough about religions other than his/her own to declare them invalid?"[24] This is a pseudoquestion. Even if one knew everything that is to be known about another religion, or even his own, he could not declare it valid or invalid, for there is no criterion for such a judgment. Smith and Burkle both imply that if one could know everything about Buddhism or Hinduism, he would know whether they are true or false. This assumption is fallacious on three counts: (1) One does not have to know everything about Nazism to know that if the beliefs and claims of Christianity are true, the beliefs and claims of Nazism are false. One does not have to know everything about the Ptolemaic worldview to know that it was basically false or incorrect. (2) Even if one knew absolutely everything about Buddhism, this in itself would tell nothing about its truth or falsity, for there is no objective criterion by which to determine the truth or falsity of its claims. (3) One could not know whether Buddhism or Hinduism are true or false, not because he lacked complete knowledge, but for the precise reason which Smith, himself, asserts: Religions are realities neither true nor false. The claims which they may make are either true or false, but not the religions themselves.

Truth of "Religious Statements"

In his discussion Smith finally gets to the point of shifting as he says, "from the truth of religion to the truth of religious statements." But his treatment is disappointing. He downgrades the importance of statements (credos) which he says are primarily the concern of us Christians and not of others. Since they are merely "our theories" they are "human constructs" whereas "Truth is divine."[25] One can be pardoned for being confused at this statement that "Truth is divine" when three pages previous to this, Smith has affirmed that "religious truth is a question of persons." Then in another place Smith says, "Theology, if we may characterize it succinctly and imperiously, is true talk about God." This *true* means "correct" and is used in the sense of the true–false dichotomy. Smith is of course free to use words in any way that he wishes, and this includes the words *true* and *truth*. What I wish he would do is to make up his mind and not confuse us with ambiguous usage. Just what is "true" talk about God? What is the criterion? As Smith uses the term one gets the feeling that it would be talk that Smith agrees with. Talk with which he does not agree would be false. This inconsistency underscores my puzzlement as to what this commodity "truth" is which religious writers bandy about so freely, whether they speak in ontological or existential terms. Truth used ontologically or existentially is a nebulous, and I believe meaningless, term. For the term to carry any concrete meaning it must be the truth about something, and therefore the truth of a statement, a claim, or a belief.

Reading Smith, it is impossible to determine whether he believes religions can or cannot be judged true or false. Such is the problem of the existential usage. Just what Smith means by "truth," or more particularly by "religious truth," is quite unclear. Yet, he is not alone in this ambiguity and impreciseness in the use of *true* and *truth*. I have analyzed Smith somewhat at length only because this confusion in the use of the words *true* and *truth* is so common among religious writers. When one reads the literature in the field he is struck constantly with the fact that those who use *truth* in either the ontological or existential sense, also revert to using it in the strictly epistemological sense of the true–false dichotomy and the confusion—if one stops to ask, "What is he really saying?"—is enormous. Writers in the field of religion—and other fields—do this without any warning that they are shifting meanings, and one wonders if they are even aware of the ambiguity themselves. In using the word *truth* in an ontological or existential sense or arguing for a particular ontological or existential usage, a writer may say, "It is true that . . . ," which is a use of *true* as the opposite of false. All the while, the writer is maintaining, theoretically at least, that truth is an ontological category and that the word *true* refers to *being* rather than to the condition or character of a statement or claim. Even the most astute writers fall into the trap. Lesslie Newbigin says,

> There is an admirable air of humility about the statement that the truth is much greater than any one person or any one religious tradition can grasp. The statement is no doubt true, but it

can be used against the truth when it is used to neutralize any
affirmation of the truth. How does the speaker know that the
truth is so much greater than this particular affirmation of it?[26]

The first *truth* is a "something" (ontological usage) that can be "great"
or "greater." The next sentence uses *true* in the true–false sense (epistemological usage). The next three times *truth* appears it is again in the
ontological sense, a "something" that can be great.

Terms Other Than *Truth* More Appropriate

My contention is that *true* and *truth* should not be used as omnibus
words carrying different meanings. In every context where these words are
used in a sense other than to indicate the opposite of false, another term
would be more appropriate, would avoid confusion, and would give a clear
and distinct meaning. For example, Smith's assertion cited above that the
claim, "The Qur'an is the word of God . . . can become true . . . that it has
become true in the life of a particular person . . . that it may become more
true for me than it yet has," would be much clearer if it read, "The Qur'an
is the word of God . . . can become meaningful . . . that it has become vital
and operative in the life of a particular person . . . and that it may become
more operative and influential for me than it yet has." "The Qur'an is the
word of God" is neither a true nor a false statement. It is a truth-claim
made by Muslims. We Christians have our own claim (and it is only a
claim) that "The Bible is the word of God." We certainly respect the claim
of Muslims, though we may or may not agree with them. Insofar as the
Qur'an and the Bible say the same thing, if either is the word of God, then
both are. But insofar as they are contradictory, they cannot be both the
word of God, unless we assume that God contradicts Himself, or that
Muslims speak of a different "God" from the one Christians speak of. The
claims of Muslims and Christians concerning the Qur'an and the Bible
involve beliefs about the nature of God. In some cases these beliefs are not
the same, but are contradictory. Simple logic decrees that if the Qur'an in
its entirety is the word of God, then the Bible in its entirety is not the word
of God or else, if indeed both are the word of God, then the God whose
word we have in the Qur'an is different from the God whose word we
have in the Bible. This, it seems to me, is simply a matter of reading and
understanding what we read.

THE EPISTEMOLOGICAL USAGE:
TRUE AS THE OPPOSITE OF *FALSE*

Truth as Those Claims about Reality Which Are Not False

I have contended that both the ontological and the existential uses of truth at best confuse and at worst distort communication. I wish now to argue that the only clear and consistent use of the word *truth* in religious discourse, and in fact in any other discourse, is the epistemological usage and that such usage properly maintained will eliminate the ambiguous ways in which the term is used, thus clarifying religious discourse, particularly in dialogue between persons of different religions. Truth in the epistemological usage is defined as "a claim about reality which is not false." In regard to the testing of such claims, the reader is referred to chapter one, where verification of both empirical and nonempirical claims is discussed.

If it were possible to turn back several thousand years, I would suggest that different terms be coined or adopted for the different usages of the word *truth*. This, however, is not a possibility. The ambiguous use of *truth* is too firmly implanted. What I propose as a practical step toward clarifying religious discourse is that in such discourse we begin to limit the use of the word *truth* to that which can be clearly shown to be not false to the satisfaction of all concerned whatever their religion. All other so-called "truths" in religious discussion would be carefully labeled "truth-claims," or "beliefs" which is in fact what they are. For who can say that it is a truth, a proven fact that God exists, or that Atman is Brahman, or that Allah is merciful, or that God was incarnate in Christ? All such claims, whether in the Jewish, Christian, Muslim, Hindu, or some other religious tradition, are just that—claims. Any one or more may turn out to be true when eschatological verification comes about. But until this comes about, they remain truth-claims.

Use of "Truth-Claims." This designation of so called "religious truths" as what they are—truth-claims—is, I believe, the only way out of the semantic muddle in which communication at times appears to take place but does not. If we are speaking of something which is claimed by some, such as a religious group or a philosophical school, to be true, as, for example, that there is a God, that Atman is Brahman, or that Allah is merciful, we should use the term *truth-claim*. The claim may be so firmly believed that for the believer it amounts to certainty—i.e., "truth." But objective appraisal will make clear that it has not been proven and in most cases cannot be proven. Thus, accurately speaking, there would be Christian truth-claims, Muslim truth-claims, Buddhist truth-claims, not Christian truths, Muslim truths, Buddhist truths. Just because a claim (belief, doctrine, etc.) may in fact be true and down the road may be so verified in terms of "eschatological verification," does not justify us in calling it a *truth*. Only that which in the present can be proven to be not false to the satisfaction of all concerned should be spoken as a truth. Even if different religions agree on certain beliefs, these beliefs are not "truths" until they have been proven to be not false to the satisfaction of all concerned.

If one objects that religious truth-claims can be and have been tested in experience and found to be true, then it must be pointed out that such proof is either strictly private or the facts involved in such proof are subject to different interpretations. These claims can be testified to; they can be proclaimed and the person testifying can show certain evidences of their truth; but they cannot be demonstrated objectively in such a way that the skeptic would have to admit that they are proven to be not false, and this is what would have to happen if they are to be declared "truths." I think I am speaking here about the simple meaning of words and what it means to communicate accurately.

Question of Criterion. A further clarification of the meaning and current usage of the word *truth* may be had by raising the question of criterion. The word *truth* carries the connotation of that which is not false. And this implies that the "truth" has met the appropriate test designed to prove that it is not false. If a "truth" is not a claim which has been established as not false, then the term loses any distinct meaning. To prove or establish a claim implies a criterion by which it is tested. So implicit in the word *truth* is the assumption that a criterion has been applied to prove that what is called "truth" is not false. A careful examination of the widespread use of the word *truth* in religious discourse will show, however, that in many cases the application of a criterion not only has not been made, but that such application is either impossible or meaningless. It is therefore my contention that religious discussion which uses the terms *true* and *truth* in this way is involved, however unintentionally, in dishonesty. This use of truth I have called the pseudo usage. The chief culprit probably is unexamined conventional usage in religious and philosophical discourse.

The difficulty created by this kind of usage is not limited to misunderstandings in interreligious dialogue. What amounts to a rather loose and careless use of the word *truth* has caused many to be justifiably skeptical. When a person talks of "truths" in religion which the listener knows are only truth-claims, the listener may be justified in raising questions as to how the word *truth* is being used, and as to whether it has any clear meaning. He may be offended by the arrogance and closed-mindedness of the speaker, or he may simply dismiss the matter as a careless kind of talk that is unworthy of serious attention.

The key factors in distinguishing a truth from a truth-claim, and thus in ferreting out improper uses of the word truth are: (1) Is the question, "The truth about what? appropriate and answerable? (2) Is the application of a criterion appropriate or indeed possible? (3) Is the criterion objective and acceptable to all concerned? Is it free of subjective opinion and feeling? If that which is spoken of as a truth has been tested and found to be not false, we have a proper use of the word. If, on the other hand, that which is spoken of as a truth is of such nature that the application of a criterion or a testing procedure is either not appropriate or not possible, or both, then we have an improper use of the word *truth*. The proper term to use in the latter case would be "belief," or "truth-claim," though I admit that the term *truth* sounds stronger and gives more status to one's beliefs. One's beliefs may be declared "truths" simply because the person knows that, though they are weak, they are of such nature that they are not falsifiable and therefore another person cannot prove them false. If, indeed the claim is not falsifiable, however, we have only an emotive statement, not an assertion to which the terms *true* or *false* are applicable.

Philosophical and Theological "Pounding the Pulpit"

One may then well ask: Why has it become so widespread as to be almost universal that religionists and many philosophers speak of religious or philosophical "truths" when what they are actually talking about are truth-claims or beliefs? Why have philosophers, theologians, and ordinary persons come to use such expressions as "the truth that God exists" or the "truth of the Incarnation"? The answer to this question seems to be that unconsciously such persons are engaging in what I speak of in chapter one as a theological or philosophical version of "pounding the pulpit." The word *truth* sounds stronger than the word *belief*. Across the ages homo convictus[27] has buttressed his metaphysical and religious claims by calling

them truths. In such usage the speaker or writer is consciously or unconsciously "pounding the pulpit" in order to make a stronger case for his
claims or beliefs. Plato (using "true" as ontologically "good") did this in the
phrase, "the good, the true, and the beautiful."

It might be noted in passing that in Plato's trilogy, "the good, the true,
and the beautiful," there is a hidden presupposition. In listing the true along
with the good and beautiful, the true is equated with the highest, the
noblest, the best. But a moment's thought will show us that the ugly, the
sordid, the despicable can be and often is also true. Unfortunately it is true
that Nazism existed and that the Nazi machine slaughtered millions of
innocent people. Do we celebrate this as "the good, the true, the beautiful"? It is true. Some would deal with this dilemma by saying that there
are different kinds of truth, but this also distorts the meaning of truth. Such
a claim is based on the ontological theory, truth being a genus with
different species. We reject this usage. Rather, the fact is that there are
different kinds of reality—good and bad, beautiful and ugly—about which
truth-claims can be made. A truth-claim is a truth-claim and, if proven not
false, is a truth regardless of the reality about which the claim is made. Truth
is truth, and thus there are no "species" of truth. There are species of reality,
and some of these species are ugly and sordid. Thus the phrase, "the good,
the true, and the beautiful" distorts the meaning of the word *true* by
implying that truth is always good and beautiful.

This kind of ambiguity, again, hampers religious dialogue. For example,
there is much that is true about Christianity that is also ugly and despicable—slave trade, imperialism, religious wars, exploitation, race prejudice,
and a host of other evils. Yet, Christians may still want to make the epistemological claim (and it is a claim, not a truth) that Jesus Christ is the
"truth" in the sense that he is, or expresses in his life, the truth about God
and human existence. They may want to claim, as I do, that living the Way
of Christ brings joy and fulfillment, but they will be careful to label this a
truth-claim and not a truth.

One may want to object that he has tested the Way of Christ in life and
has found it true. I agree. As a Christian I have personally made such a test
and find that the Way of Christ is in total harmony with reality as I experience it, and in this sense expresses the truth about reality. It is in this sense
that I speak of Jesus as "the Truth." But I must admit that though I believe
it with all my heart and find it proven in daily life to my own satisfaction,

it is not "proven" in an objective scientific sense. Others might want to dispute the claim, and I must admit that the claim not having been objectively proven to the satisfaction of all concerned, thus remains my truth-claim, however firmly I believe it is true. If we can once reach the point of removing the arrogance, however unintentional, that is involved when we talk about the "truths" of this religion or that, and recognize that all of us are talking about truth-claims or beliefs, however convinced we are that they are in fact true, we will have made significant progress in interreligious relationships. Also, it should now be clear why we reject the term "true religion."

What about Revelation?

One other question must be considered here. Many will ask, "But what about the matter of revelation?" Some religions claim that they in no sense simply express truth-claims because the "truths" they have are revealed to them. To admit that what they express are merely human truth-claims would be to deny the essence of their faith, which is that they have the truth because it comes directly from God by revelation and therefore must be true. How are we to deal with this objection?

The answer is not as difficult as it may seem. The fact is that the claim to have "revelation" is just that—a claim. Persons making this claim have not and cannot get an Archimedean position outside of the world, a vantage point independent of human existence from which they can know independent of any possible human failing that their "revelation" is directly from God. So whether they wish to admit it or not, all they have is a human truth-claim—namely the claim that they have revelation. They may wish to stake their lives on this claim, but it is, nevertheless, a claim, a belief. If they claim that what they hold is absolute truth because it is in the Bible or in the Qur'an or in some other scripture and therefore must be God's word, it must be pointed out that the claim or belief that the Bible or the Qur'an or some other scripture is God's word, is a human claim or a human belief, even though the Bible or the Qur'an may say so. I, for example, believe that the Bible is the Word of God. But I cannot escape the dilemma that a person's choice of allegiance to Christianity, to Islam, or to whatever, and the choice of an authority—that is, the belief that what the Bible says, or what the Qur'an says, or what some other authority says, is God's word—is a human choice or a human claim or a human belief, for after all, we are human. In each case it is what we believe to be true. I do not minimize in any way the importance of such belief. For example, for me such belief is utterly crucial, a matter of life and death, and I do stake my life on it. But it is still a belief, not a truth, even though I, of course, believe it is true.

Concern with Accurate Communication

Again, I wish to stress that my primary concern here is not with the precision of language for language's sake or with nit-picking usages of the word *truth*. Rather it is a concern for accurate communication, which, with a generous helping of goodwill and tact, can go a long way toward overcoming the present tensions, and sometimes hostility, that exist in interreligious circles. I am advocating the use of the term *truth* exclusively for that which can be shown to be not false to the satisfaction of all concerned, which is, after all, in my judgment, the real meaning of the term. Everything else would be termed a truth-claim or belief. This practice would eliminate what I have called the existential and the ontological usages of truth. In this sense, when Jesus is spoken of as "the Truth," (quoting scripture) Christians would understand and make clear that this is their truth-claim, their belief in the Bible. It is their truth-claim that in Jesus' life, teaching, death, and resurrection one finds the truth about God and human existence. We looked in some detail at the "scientific" evidence for this "truth-claim" in chapter one. It is simply a testimony to personal experience, and in no sense an argument. We would in no sense claim superiority, better, best, only, final, etc. Christians would simply express their belief and their experience and proclaim: "*Ecce Homo*—Behold the man!" In interreligious relationships there is no problem in making such a testimony loud and clear so long as it is a testimony to experience and not an arrogant assertion of some supposed sacrosanct "truth." It is a truth-claim on which the Christian stands firmly but humbly, and in openness to the total religious experience of the human race. Such an approach in no way undermines the zeal and commitment of the Christian. But it does set his life-commitment to Jesus Christ as Savior and Lord in its proper interreligious context.

The kind of reevaluation of the use of the word *truth* which I am suggesting here will not be easy. However, with the wave of the future in the direction of increasing religious pluralism, and with the increasing need for dialogue, it may not be too vain a hope that one day, at least in interreligious discourse, we will begin to use more accurate and less emotionally charged terminology. As to terminology which might express what has been intended by the ontological and existential uses of *true* and *truth* in religious discourse, we might try such terms as *real* or *reality*, *essence*, or *real essence*, *authentic*, *authentic existence*, *genuine*, *genuine personhood*, etc., depending on the context.[28] There are many other possibilities. Truth-claims in the form of beliefs, doctrines, values, etc. could then be freely discussed among the adherents of different religions as human beings, with no one feeling that the other had arrogated to himself or herself the claim that he/she had "the truth" in regard to nonempirical, non-verifiable beliefs and values. Values, beliefs could be shared to the enrichment of all. The essence of what I am proposing was suggested many years ago by the late E. Stanley Jones in his *Christ At the Round Table*.[29] The "Round Table," whether literal or figurative, was to symbolize that each of the adherents of the different religions was in an equal position in relation to all the others, and together they discussed their commitments. The focus was on testimony and not on claims. Beliefs were discussed only in relation to how they worked out in daily living. Argument was not allowed, and neither was preaching. Each one witnessed to his own faith, asked, and answered questions. We will refer to this method again in chapter six, when we speak about contemporary Christian mission in the twenty-first century.

Chapter Three
OFFER THEM CHRIST

THE LIFE

IN THE LAST CHAPTER WE DISCUSSED THE QUESTION OF "TRUTH." WE closed with an emphasis on interreligious dialogue centered around personal religious experience, not around discussing or arguing beliefs and doctrines as such. For the Christian, personal experience is always centered in Jesus Christ. Therefore, Christian evangelism, properly understood, has always been centered in Jesus Christ and not in such things as arguments as to which is the true religion or which religion will get one to heaven. In an age of religious pluralism the necessity of making clear this centering in Jesus Christ is even more urgent. For this reason, the question of the relationship of the Christian faith to other religions must be seen as primarily a question of Christology, and Christian mission must be seen as primarily a matter of "Offering them Christ," presenting them a life, a living person. Remember, Jesus said, "I am the Way, the Truth, and the Life" (John 14:6). The response of the Christian faith to the ideology of religious pluralism centers in Christology. Therefore, in speaking of evangelism in an age of religious pluralism we must deal with the question: What kind of Christology will provide the basis for a sound, reasonable, vigorous, and effective evangelism in a world that from a religious point of view is becoming increasingly pluralistic, and in a society where the controlling ideology is increasingly becoming the ideology of religious pluralism? This Christology in my judgment must be one that centers not on "religion" or on beliefs or doctrines, even the doctrine of Incarnation, but on the person, Jesus Christ, himself, risen and living today in person, the Lord of the universe.

Broadly speaking, two types of Christology have provided, for the most part, the theological foundation for the Christian missionary enterprise: Incarnational Christology and *Logos* Christology. Though there are many variations of each of these, we will look at each as a type of Christology. Incarnational Christology has focused on the historic person of Jesus as the "enfleshment" of God in a particular time and place and person. It has placed great emphasis on the actual historic event in which God was for thirty-three years incarnate in a human being, Jesus of Nazareth. Salvation is understood to be through faith in this Jesus, who in a specific time and place came to live among us, to teach, preach, heal, and to die on the cross for our sins. The view which I will present below starts with the Incarnation and is founded upon it. It assumes the deity of Jesus Christ, the virgin birth, the death on the cross for our redemption, and the other beliefs of orthodox Christology. But it seeks to develop this Christology further and to place the focus on the risen and living person, Jesus Christ, in a more explicit way both in terms of Christology and soteriology.

Logos Christology, on the other hand, has focused not on the Incarnation, but on the Greek concept of *Logos*. The use of the term *Logos* in Christian theology comes primarily through John 1:14 which says, "And the Word [*Logos*] became flesh . . . " Across the years there has been considerable disagreement as to the way in which the term *Logos* in John's Gospel is to be interpreted. Should it be seen basically in terms of the Greek usage of the term, or should the parallelism to Genesis 1:1 be the key? Both John and Genesis open with the phrase, "In the beginning." Genesis says, "In the beginning, God . . . " John definitely equates the *Logos* with God: "The *Logos* was God." This verse tends to support the view that the usage in John is Hebrew—that is, that it presupposes the Hebrew understanding of deity as a personal being, rather than the Greek understanding of deity as an impersonal philosophical absolute. If we follow J. A. T. Robinson's suggestion that John's Gospel comes out of an early—prior to the Jewish revolt in A.D. 66–70—Palestinian milieu rather than a later Greek milieu, then the use of *Logos* is not to be understood in a Greek philosophical context.[1] Bultmann also suggests that the term *Logos* as used by John comes out of a non-Greek mythological tradition and that the usage is Hebrew and not Greek.[2]

To enter into this exegetical debate is beyond the scope of this essay. Suffice it to say that the *Logos* Christology which has been prominent in missiology and which in the present day is being seen to be compatible with the ideology of religious pluralism is based primarily on the Greek philosophical concept of *Logos*. This *Logos* Christology has focused not on the historic event of the Incarnation, the thirty-three years of Jesus' life on earth—though it certainly does not deny this—but on the universal "spirit" or "*Logos*" which it holds has existed from eternity, has been manifest in many ways among peoples all over the earth, and has found its most important and decisive expression in the person of Jesus Christ.

These two views with a number of variations have persisted through the centuries. In the *Logos* view, the Universal *Logos*, is thought to have entered the human Jesus and in some sense to have formed his essential nature. The exact relationship of the divine *Logos* to the human Jesus has been vigorously debated from the early days of the church. However, in one way or another the *Logos* is seen as having been in a special way present in the earthly Jesus for thirty-three years while at the same time remaining the Universal Spirit or *Logos* present everywhere. Another way to express it is that the *Logos* is thought in some sense to have constituted the personhood of Jesus while at the same time continuing to be universal in the world (God). Thus in this sense one might say that the *Logos* incarnate in Jesus was only part of the Universal *Logos*, but the part which was in him was constitutive of Jesus' personality in such a special and complete way that Jesus was the special and complete revelation of God.

Likewise, it should be noted that *Logos* Christology has sometimes been developed along lines that have made only slight, if any, reference to Jesus of Nazareth. Some philosophically-oriented approaches speak of Christ in such abstract and universal terms that whether there is any connection between Christ and the concrete, human Jesus of Nazareth is questionable. For example, Jesus is seen as "the Christ" in Tillich's theology, but the way Tillich speaks of and develops "the Christ" as "transparent symbol" leaves only marginal connection, if any, to an actual historical person who lived in Nazareth. Likewise, for John Cobb "Christ" is seen as the "principle of creative transformation," and the connection with Jesus of Nazareth, if any, is quite vague.

It is easy to see that this *Logos* Christology is much less restrictive than Incarnational Christology. If the *Logos*, which is universal, is indeed "the Christ," then Christ is everywhere in all cultures and all religions. Current examples of this *Logos* Christology are found in Raymond Panikkar's *The Unknown Christ of Hinduism*,[3] and John Cobb's *Christ In a Pluralistic Age*.[4] Though *Logos* Christology takes a number of forms and though the way in which the *Logos* is present outside of Christianity may be viewed differently by different writers, the fact of its presence in some way in the persons, in the religions, or in the cultures is affirmed by those affirming this type of Christology. It is this type of Christology which is affirmed by those in the current scene who are seeking to develop what they call a "universal theology of religion."[5] They operate entirely on the basis of a unitarian, philosophical concept of God, and the *logos* is a spirit or some kind of impersonal manifestation of this unitarian God. Those wishing to affirm faith in Christ as the source of salvation and yet avoid the arrogance of exclusivism which they believe is inherent in Incarnational Christology, have uniformly developed some form of the *Logos* Christology.

While the problem with *logos* Christology may be that it is too broad, has too little connection with Jesus of Nazareth, and thus removes the uniqueness of the Christian faith, the problem with an Incarnational Christology is that it can become too much bound to past history—to a time and a place. It is this kind of "history-bound" Christology which Rudolph Bultmann sought to eliminate in his existentialist "demythologizing" by bringing the "Christ event" into the present experience of the individual. An incarnational Christology can so focus on first century Palestine that it renders Christ quite irrelevant to other times and places. Likewise, it can tend toward narrow exclusiveness at the institutional and doctrinal level. As Pawlikowski points out, "Too often Incarnational Christology has led to anti-social attitudes on the part of Christians."[6]

A *Logos* Christology, on the other hand, tends to reduce Christ to a universal spirit or to a kind of universal principle. This in final analysis reduces him either to an idea or an ideal, that is, to a kind of force abroad in the world. A principal or a force is an "it," and one will note that the *logos* is referred to as an "it" in most discourse. Certainly a metaphysical force may be an important reality in the sense of shared values, but it cannot be the ontological reality we speak of as the person, Jesus Christ. We cannot limit Christ to one time and place—rigid Incarnational Christology—the resurrection forbids it. Neither can we reduce him to an impersonal force in the world—*Logos* Christology—however "personal" (whatever that may mean) this force may be seen to be in various "incarnations" or manifestations, as Raymond Panikkar and John B. Cobb suggest. In the attempt to avoid exclusivism, much contemporary Christology is moving toward complete relativism as is seen in the recent books, *No Other Name?*, *The Myth of Christian Uniqueness,* and *Toward a Universal Theology of Religion.*[7] The question, then, is what kind of Christology will both do justice to the uniqueness of Jesus Christ and at the same time avoid exclusivism and narrowness? In this chapter we will seek to develop such a Christology. Before taking up our constructive effort, however, we will look at two contemporary *Logos* Christologies which seek to deal with the issue of the Christian faith and religious pluralism.

CURRENT *LOGOS* CHRISTOLOGIES

Wolfhart Pannenberg

A number of twentieth century contributions to Christology that impinge on the relationship of Christianity to other religions are emerging out of various aspects of Jesus studies which profess to go beyond both the liberals' surrender of all uniqueness for Jesus on the one hand, and the rigid claims to exclusivism made by classical orthodox theologians and modern Barthians on the other hand. One of these is Wolfhart Pannenberg. To prepare for a development of what I will call a "Person Christology," I want to examine briefly his proposals.

Pannenburg seeks to avoid the relativism of Troeltsch and the exclusivism of Barth. In his theology of history he sees Jesus Christ as unique but unique only as a revelation within history which also includes the history of other religions. The revelation in Jesus Christ is the "prolepsis" of God's total revelation in the history of mankind. Pannenberg says "Only through Jesus does it become clear what the God of Israel really is and means."[8] He affirms God's revelation in other religious traditions. Revelation is seen as facts or truths about God which are revealed. The revelation in Jesus is the full and complete revelation within history, the norm and prolepsis of God's action in all of history. God is the God of history and his presence in man's religious dimension is a form of universal divine revelation. As will be readily seen, Pannenberg's view is simply one form of the traditional *Logos* Christology in which there is the "general revelation" of God—the *Logos* present with and in all men and all religions—while Jesus Christ is the "special revelation," the *Logos* made flesh, in a special way. Jesus Christ is the central manifestation of the *Logos* in concrete history. Pannenberg says

> Jesus of Nazareth is the final revelation of God because the end
> of history appeared in him. It did so both in his eschatological

message and in his resurrection from the dead. However, he can
be understood to be God's final revelation only in connection
with the whole of history as mediated by the history of Israel.
He is God's revelation in the fact that all history receives its light
from him. [9]

In calling Jesus of Nazareth "the final revelation," Pannenberg implies
a relativity. Jesus is the last in a series, not the unique Son of God. Also
Pannenberg does not seem to be troubled by the assumption that he
somehow has achieved a vantage point outside of history, from which
vantage point he has a criterion for judging that Jesus Christ is the "final
revelation" and the "end of history." Pannenberg falls into the subtle trap,
seemingly without realizing it, that any comparison—superior, better, best,
highest, final, etc.—implies an objective criterion which in the nature of
the case does not exist. That there can be criteria we admit. In fact there
are absolutes, as we indicate elsewhere. But such criteria are faith statements or assumptions and can only serve as a basis for the declaration
"final" or "highest" or "best" from an individual personal faith perspective
with which another may disagree. They are in no sense obvious universal
criteria affirmed by all. Therefore, the terms "final revelation" and "end of
history" are not indicative statements but can only function as evocative
expressions such as "Praise God," expressing how Pannenberg feels.

Pannenberg adopts what he calls an inductive method in developing
his Christology. He holds that the recognition of Jesus' divinity is the result
of Jesus' life, death, and resurrection—primarily the resurrection, which
Pannenberg, in opposition to Bultmann and the existentialists, holds can be
proven historically. While seeking to avoid Barth's exclusivism, Pannenberg
nevertheless holds to a kind of exclusivism in that he insists on the finality
of the revelation in Christ. In him God's ultimate will and final purpose
for all history are seen proleptically as the "end of history."

From the above, it will be clear that Pannenberg's Christology suffers
from the same kind of superiority complex as the other twentieth century
views which see Christ as the "crown" or the "fulfillment" of other religions.
When Pannenberg says that the Christ-event is an event for all peoples, since
in Christ "God is finally and fully revealed" and that "no further revelation
of God can happen,"[10] he expresses not only a superiority claim, but also

subtly implies that he actually knows what the full and complete revelation is apart from Christ—else how could he judge that the revelation in Christ is the final one? How can I know that a given animal is a real elephant unless I know what an elephant is?

Possibly Pannenberg's error is that he is not inductive enough—or that he does not stay consistently with his inductive method. If one is consistently inductive, possibly all he can say out of his own encounter with Jesus Christ, out of his own inner life-transforming experience is: *Ecce Homo*—"Behold the Man." He can testify to Christ as his own Savior and Lord, but the moment he begins to make claims based on comparisons—i.e., highest, best, final, normative, complete, etc.—he makes a claim to have an Archimedian vantage point outside of human existence, to know more than he can possibly know since he is not himself in possession of superior knowledge or an absolute criterion by which he can judge the quality of the revelation in Christ in comparison with other revelations, if there be such. Certainly one is entitled to make these assertions—highest, best, final, etc. as personal testimonies or faith statements expressing personal experience and personal commitment, but if they are made as "truth-claims" he must recognize that he does not and cannot have an objective vantage point from which vantage point he has a criterion by which such claims can be substantiated.

Pannenberg's "historical" Christology, therefore, breaks down at the point of supplying us a view or an approach which can take into account what Christians feel they must maintain concerning the uniqueness of Jesus Christ, and at the same time avoid the superiority claim. Lucien Richard criticizes Pannenberg, claiming that "he has not been able to bring about a middle of the road approach, a concept of Christianity which would bring out clearly its fundamental distinctions from other religions and yet show that this distinction does not set Christianity completely above other traditions."[11] Then Richard asks, "Cannot God in his universal salvific will make us aware of other salvific mediations besides that of the humanity of Jesus? Must the encounter with God's love which is a salvific encounter be necessarily related to Jesus of Nazareth?"[12] Such a question shows clearly that Richard rejects the Incarnation and the uniqueness of Jesus. It presupposes a unitarian, not a trinitarian concept God, and Richard clearly comes down on the side of relativism. In this approach, God is not incarnate in Jesus of Nazareth in the sense of the Christian doctrine of Trinity, but could be incarnate in other "salvific mediations" as in the various Indian or Hindu avatars. Jesus Christ is not an inherent and integral part of the Godhead, as the Christian doctrine of Trinity affirms.

John B. Cobb Jr.

Another contemporary approach to the issue is that of John B. Cobb. Cobb's book, *Christ In a Pluralistic Age*, develops a *Logos* Christology in Whiteheadian terms, and this Christology, he believes, is adequate to meet the needs of the current pluralistic age. In Cobb's view, the Incarnation is seen in terms of a complete embodiment of the *Logos* in Jesus of Nazareth. The *Logos* is the "essential self" of Jesus. The human "I" in him is identical with the immanent *Logos*: "In Jesus there is a distinctive incarnation because his very selfhood was constituted by the *Logos*."[13] Actually Cobb's view is not too different from that first advanced by Apollinarius in the fourth century. Apollinarius held that the divine *Logos* simply inhabited the human body of Jesus which implied that Jesus was neither fully human nor fully divine. He was simply a divine being masquerading in a human body. This view has been rejected by the predominant stream of Christian theology. We agree with Alan Richardson when he says, "The church was right in rejecting the theory of Apollinarius. Jesus becomes an inexplicable enigma unless he is in the fullest sense human."[14] Also in Cobb's view, the *Logos*, though concentrated in Jesus, is present in lesser degree everywhere. He says, "The *Logos* is incarnate in all human beings and indeed in all creation."[15] Therefore, "To assert that the *Logos* was incarnate in Jesus in itself . . . is true but insufficient."[16] Jesus Christ is only a "paradigm case of incarnation." Cobb's focus is on the *Logos*, and for him "Christ" is equated with the *Logos* in the world. "Christ" is defined as the force of "creative transformation" in the world. This "creative transformation" is the *Logos* or the Christ at work in all of culture through all of history.

As already indicated, we must reject this *Logos* Christology. That Jesus Christ has had a powerful influence in the world, causing a tremendously creative transformation of society across history is obvious. Jesus Christ has truly been a "creative transformer" of culture. But this transformation has been effected by Jesus Christ as a person, relating as a person to other persons in the world, not as a nebulous "*Logos*" or impersonal spirit in the world. It is Jesus Christ as a person who has set these forces in motion in the world. That there are spiritual forces turned loose in the world through both the earthly Jesus of history and the risen Lord, is again clearly attested. But these forces have no ontological reality apart from Jesus himself or the individuals whose personal existence has been challenged and changed by the person, Jesus Christ, and who therefore have exerted these forces in the world. The force and influence of Jesus' personality may be spoken of as the *Logos* if we wish, but this is an entirely different thing. Unless we stick strictly with John's Gospel and use the term *Logos* as a synonym for God, "The *Logos* was God" (John 1:1), the *Logos* as a supposed ontological "something" has no independent existence. "*Logos*," used in this way, is simply a universal idea or concept which has existence only in the minds of persons conceiving of it. Ontological reality, we will seek to maintain, falls into two categories: (1) "person" and (2) "thing" or what I am calling "nonperson." All ontological reality is either one or the other. If the reality is not a person or persons, as we will define person, it is nonperson or a thing or things. We will look at this ontology in more detail as we proceed.

PERSON CHRISTOLOGY

The foregoing discussion provides a background for our constructive effort to develop what I will call a "Person Christology." This Christology which focuses on the living Jesus, (who is the Way, the Truth, and the Life) might also be thought of as a "Resurrection Christology" in that it puts major emphasis on the resurrected and living person, Jesus Christ. But I prefer the term "Person Christology." In fact, it is a Person Christology precisely because it focuses on Jesus Christ as a resurrected and living person today, not on the traditional issues that have characterized Christology, as stated earlier. It assumes the Incarnation and the deity of Jesus, but goes on to focus on Jesus as a resurrected person, living today. The existentialist and other personalistic emphases which have come to have a prominent place in twentieth century thought point in my judgment to the emphases I will make here and indeed these movements together with the modern understanding of the person seem to make a Person Christology compelling.

The Term *Person*

In using the term, *Person Christology,* I will need initially to do two things. First, I will need to deal with the charge that the term, *person,* is too anthropomorphic to use in referring to God. Paul Tillich and others reject the use of the term *person* and opt for use of the term *personal* in referring to God. John Hick says, "Most phrases [using the term *person*] suggest the picture of a magnified human individual."[17] Certainly many think of God in anthropomorphic terms as an old man in the sky with long white hair and a long white beard. But this need not be so in speaking of God as the Divine Person. Alan Richardson says, "Personality implies limitation: the self implies the not-self, and infinite personality [a self without a not-self] seems a contradiction in terms."[18] However, it seems to me that if God is not a person (Divine Person) over against the world, then all we have is pantheism, which clearly seems to be the direction of Tillich (ground of being) and others in this tradition of "Identity."

In regard to the contention of Tillich, Hick, Richardson, and others, I see no way in which the term *person* is more anthropomorphic than the term *personal.* The way in which reality could be personal and not a person escapes me. If personal is not an adjective which describes an attribute or attributes of a person, then what does it mean? Of course the motive of Tillich and Hick is to make clear that God is not "a magnified human being." Yet, to avoid giving way completely to the via negativa, they say that God is at least personal, but is *more* than personal. he is suprapersonal. But if this is true, God is still a person, only a type of person superior to a human person. Alan Richardson says, "It may . . . be objected that this [the term suprapersonal] again makes God an unknown and unknowable transcendent being, like the God of Greek philosophy." Richardson then answers the objection by pointing out that "by saying that God is suprapersonal we do not thereby imply that he is not personal."[19]

I see no reason, therefore, to deny the use of the term *person* when speaking of God. Tillich, Richardson, and Hick simply have too narrow a definition of person when they confine it to the human sphere. There is no reason why person cannot apply to the divine as well as to the human. As we will seek to show below there are only two categories of ontological reality, namely that which is a person or persons, and that which is not a person or persons, namely a thing or things. There are two categories of person: the Divine Person and human persons, and possibly an intermediary category such as angels and demons. Understood in this way and in

terms of our definition of person in this chapter, I see no problem whatever in using the term *person* for God. In fact, considering the ontology
presented here, I think it is mandatory. Otherwise, "God" is simply a
thing—a kind of "world soul" or, in Hindu terms, a "Brahma"—an "it."

Second, we will need to distinguish between the modern use of the
term *person*, and the classical use in the creeds of the church. The Latin
word *persona* which is used in the creeds referred not to an individual
person in the modern sense—a unitary center of self consciousness—but
to the role or function an individual played in society. Hence its use in the
theater in relation to a mask worn by an actor playing different parts in a
drama. It is in this sense that Tertullian speaks of the Trinity as *una
substantia, tres personae.* We wish to leave this classical usage behind and turn
to the contemporary usage of the term *person.* We believe that a full understanding of this modern usage opens the possibility of giving a new focus
to Christology and opens a way for a better understanding of Jesus Christ,
who he was and is and what he has accomplished and still accomplishes.

The terms *person, personality,* and *personhood,* as used today, refer to
the most mysterious reality in a world of ever increasing mysteries. The
more we learn about the world in which we live, both the "microcosm"
and the "macrocosm," the more mystery we find. The discovery of the
atomic structure of matter explains many things, but deepens the mystery
of many others. The more space vehicles probe outer space, the more we
learn. But also the more mystery we uncover. The more psychologists
study the human person, the more we learn, but also the more complex
the mystery of personhood becomes. The more both philosophy and
psychology study the mind, the more we know and yet the more we
know that we do not know. Freud, Jung, Adler, Frankl, and others have
shed much light, but the more the light shines, the deeper the mystery
becomes. There is the mystery of the uniqueness and the absolute
privacy of the human mind. No one can probe a person's mind unless
that person communicates his or her thoughts or feelings in some way.
There is the mystery of self-transcendence—that we cannot only be the
subject in our thinking, but also the object of our thinking. There is the
mystery of human freedom. So long as the mind remains human (unal-
tered by drugs or psychological pressures) it cannot be forced against the
will. Galileo, forced by the church to recant his claim that the earth
moves around the sun, mutters under his breath, "But it does move."
One cannot be forced to think untrue something he knows is true. Yet,

one must also recognize the interrelationship of mental functioning with the physiology of the body, seen particularly in cases where psychological and mental functioning is gravely affected by inherited or acquired imbalance of body chemistry.

There is the mystery of the social nature of human personhood, for human personhood only comes into being in the context of society—mother, child, family, etc. Though strictly private, as just pointed out, it is also of necessity social. There is the mystery of interpersonal relationships and the influence of one person on another; there is the mystery of love, hate, compassion, and other emotions. There is the mystery of the conscious mind—unconscious mind (or subconscious mind) relationship, both a duality and a unity. There is the mystery of awareness which can obliterate time and space, removing such distinctions as past, present, and future. There is the mystery of what Martin Buber calls the "I–Thou" relationship, which not only alters the subject–object split in a significant way, but also alters the "I" in a qualitative way: The I in the I–Thou relationship is different from the I in the I–it relationship. It can also alter the "Thou." Put together with all of these mysteries the mysteries of unusual talents and abilities, extrasensory perception, what we call dual or multiple personalities in one person, and other non-typical features that are sometimes found in the human person, and we begin to see that the complexities and intricacies are almost infinite.

The tremendously wide range of experiences, insights, and capabilities of the human person is underscored again by the wide range of genius that is frequently found in "savants." Consider, for example Leslie Lemke.[20] Because of a birth injury he was born blind and retarded with cerebral palsy. Yet, he can hear a complicated piece of music he has never heard before such as Debussy's "Soiree Dans Grenade," then sit down immediately at the piano and play it in its entirety. No matter how long the piece he can play all of it on hearing it for the first time. Or consider Alonzo Clements, a "retarded" person who cannot count much beyond ten, but who can simply see an animal, go to his home, and carve an accurate, artful statue of the animal. Then, there is George Finn, a forty-three-year-old patient at the Brown Psychiatric Rehabilitation Center. His mind is a kind of history computer. He can instantly tell the day of the week any date in history fell on or will fall on. For example, when asked what day of the week May 30, A.D. 1 fell on or what day of the week February 3, A.D. 2065 will be on, he instantly gives the correct answer. What years in the past twenty-five has

September 1st come on Friday? Finn: 1961, 1967, 1972, 1978. He is always right. He cannot tell anyone how he does it. He just does it.

My point is not to focus on these unusual aberrations of human consciousness or human abilities, or to suggest that they in themselves mean anything special or that they prove any particular point. My point is simply to stress the fantastic diversity and almost infinite variety and possibilities of the person even at the human level and of personhood as such, either human or divine. If we assume that there is a divine person, God, and I do, the almost infinite possibilities of personhood as such (human or divine) become actually infinite. If we focus on "person" as such and the infinite possibilities this reality possesses and not on "human" and "divine," we get a totally different perspective on the possibility of Incarnation. A person fully human and also fully divine is in this sense not an impossibility at all. Though from the point of view of human logic, the human person, limited by time and space, and the divine person, unlimited by any factors, may appear to be contradictories, such may not actually be the case at all if we focus on the ontological reality we call "person." The same human limitations that make such a reality appear contradictory may be the limitations that prevent us from seeing the real nature of reality, namely that such a "divine–human" reality is not self-contradictory. Our problem may be with the categories of human thought and the limitations of human logic, not with the reality itself.[21] That one person, Jesus Christ, could be both divine and human is therefore not so incredible, but is definitely within the range of possibility if we are not locked into the Greek metaphysical contradictories which make such a being a logical impossibility. It is my contention that the ontological reality called *person* when seen in its real nature, whether at the divine or the human level, is quite capable of providing an ontological basis for the Christian doctrine of Incarnation and Trinity, and for Jesus Christ as the Absolute Person, as the revelation of reality, the revelation of God as he is and humanity as created to be. Actually, we believe we are not too far from the basic views of Augustine as expressed in his analogies of the Trinity.

There are of course still logical problems and we in no sense suggest that this view "explains" the Incarnation and the Trinity, for they are and will remain, from a human perspective—that is human logic—mysteries beyond human comprehension. But the Incarnation need not be ruled out as simply impossible. Many theologians have sought to throw light on the mystery of the Incarnation, and we will not attempt to go into these proposals. However, one important suggestion in recent months has been that of Thomas V. Morris in his book, *The Logic of God Incarnate*.[22]

Morris proposes what he calls a "Two Minds" Christology and points to the complexity of the reality we call person. He prefers the term *mind*, however, and speaks of two minds, one human and one divine, in Jesus Christ. He believes that the Kenotic theory of God emptying himself to become human has much to commend it, but believes that his "two-minds" theory is better. He gives several analogies: (1) The distinction in conscious mind and subconscious (or unconscious) mind in the same person. (2) Two computer programs, one containing but not contained by the other; (3) The dreamer, who takes part in his dream "from the inside" while at the same time as sleeper "is somehow aware . . . [from the outside] that it is just a dream that is going on."[23] I would suggest another phenomenon much more common, it seems to me, which is simply the fact of self-transcendence. There is the mind that is thinking and the mind that transcends the thinking mind and "sees" or is aware of the thinking mind. In other words, one thinks about the thinking mind or the thinking person.

Yet, it is one person or one mind. This phenomenon as well as those suggested by Morris are, however, in my view, not so much evidence of "two minds" as they are of the fantastic complexity and infinite possibilities of the person. Once we recognize the possibilities inherent in the ontological reality we call *person*, whether in the human or the divine mode, the seeming impossibilities—actually due to our own definitions and use of dualistic and inappropriate Greek philosophical terms in speaking of the Incarnation—disappear.

Morris's discussion is quite helpful. However, the focus on "mind" seems in the first place to be too narrow, for a person is more than a mind. There is the emotion, the will, creativity, imagination, etc. In the second place, it tends, in the tradition of certain ancient "heresies," to split the personality of Jesus, though Morris denies this. Morris is either not far from Apollinarianism, though for him there is both a divine mind and a human mind in Jesus, or else his view is subject to the charge of split personality. Person Christology as I conceive it, using the richer and broader concept of person, leaves open the specific way in which Jesus is the divine–human person because the ontological reality we speak of as person—particularly in the divine manifestation—is too complex and is certainly beyond our human comprehension. Yet, Person

Christology believes that it points clearly and reasonably to the distinct possibility of the divine–human person.

Taking the Resurrection Seriously

The Person Christology I am proposing obviously takes the resurrection of Jesus seriously. The question that has emerged in our modern scientific age, faced so squarely by Rudolf Bultmann, is: "Was the resurrection of Jesus an event in the history of Jesus, or was it only an event in the experience of the first disciples?" A large segment of New Testament scholarship in the twentieth century has come to accept the latter view, and speaks of the resurrection as the "Easter Faith." There are notable exceptions, but by and large the view expounded so effectively by Bultmann seems to have become the view accepted by liberal theologians as consistent with the modern scientific worldview. With the resurrection thus reduced to a psychological event in human experience, the only sense in which we can speak of the risen, living Christ is as he lives in our experience. Jesus Christ, living today as a person independent of our human experience disappears.

Person Christology takes direct opposition to this Bultmanian view. It affirms the resurrection as an objective event, something that happened in the history of Jesus—not something that happened in the experience of the disciples only—and that happens in our experience today. Person Christology as understood here is possible on the basis of the dualistic ontology affirmed in this essay, namely the ontological reality of both persons and that which is not person, which we speak of as "things." Person Christology affirms the present reality of the resurrected, living person, Jesus Christ, rather than the continuing presence of a vague impersonal "spirit" or *logos* dispersed throughout the world. Classical Christologies assumed the resurrection of Jesus in a literal sense, and likewise a number of current Christologies, such as that of Wolfhart Pannenberg, view the resurrection as a real event in the history of Jesus, and thus affirm his living presence in the world today. But in a large part of the theological reflection in the last half of the twentieth century, the resurrection has not been taken with sufficient seriousness and consistency in terms of its implications for Jesus as a living person today, independent of the existence of the church or of personal religious experience. If Jesus is truly risen, as we believe he is, he is alive today as a person, not as a *logos*, or as an "Easter faith" on the part of his disciples, whether of the first century or the twentieth. He is alive as a noncorporeal person, for he is God, the second person of the Trinity, and we must spell out the meaning of this assertion and the meaning of a Christology based on it. This I hope to do in terms of both ontology and soteriology.

A segment of twentieth century theology a few years ago witnessed the complete abandonment of belief in the resurrection in what came to be known as the "Death of God" theology. The logical conclusion of Paul Tillich's concept of God as the "Ground of Being" is the "Death of God" theology, and Thomas Altizer is reported to have said this in an address where he and Tillich appeared together on the same platform. Altizer believes that the resurrection is the cardinal heresy of the Christian church. This heresy, according to Altizer, has blocked the full completion of the Christian faith in history because it has blocked the complete secularization of human existence. The doctrine of resurrection has prevented the complete acceptance by Christians of the demise of deity, which Altizer insists is a reality.

However, the "Death of God" theology has not prevailed. There are still Christologies which assume a "presence" of Christ today in some sense other than the Death of God's "died into the world" and "man for others" concepts. Karl Rahner expresses the sense of the presence of Jesus as living person today. He speaks of "the individual Christian's personal relationship with Jesus" and points to the validity of maintaining a living relationship with "those who have left our own circle and have entered the silent eternity of God." He then concludes: "If this is correct in general, it is also correct when it is applied to the particular relationship that we can and ought to have with the living Jesus."[24]

Yet, it appears that Rahner does not actually take the resurrection with sufficient theological seriousness as regards its rather clear implication that unless Jesus has somehow "died" again, he is a living person today in his own right as a person, and not merely as a function of the church or of human consciousness. If Jesus actually rose from the dead, he is alive as a person today in and of himself and in no way is dependent for his existence on whether anyone or any community believes he is alive. It is puzzling, then, when Rahner says, "If there were no community of faith until the end of time consisting of those who believed in Jesus as the crucified and risen Christ, the saved [sic] Son of God and the unique, definitive and eschatological prophet (however this may be formulated), there would be no permanent presence of God in the world and Jesus would not be present as God's promise of himself."[25] Rahner's strong Ecclesiology is apparent here. From the perspective of Person Christology, however, Jesus as a risen living person is present in his own existence, not as a feature of a community of faith.

If Jesus as a person really rose from the dead and is today a living, though noncorporeal person, would he not be "present" (in so far as this term may apply analogically to a noncorporeal person) whether there is a church or not? Rahner talks of the personal presence of Jesus, but he obviously means something different from the presence of a person in and of himself, which if such presence is a reality would not be dependent on the existence of the church or anything else. We may speak of the church as a witness to this presence, but not as the presence itself. Schoonenberg uses the term "Presence Christology," but it lacks the central focus on the Person, Jesus Christ, which is the cornerstone of Person Christology. As Bernard Ramm points out, the doctrine of *Christus Praesens* has almost dropped out of theological literature.[26]

Resurrection and *Logos* Christology

In terms of the missiological issue with which we are dealing here, namely the relationship of the uniqueness of Christ to his universality, if theologians had taken seriously Jesus Christ's living presence as a person—the true meaning of the resurrection—they would not have felt the need for a "*Logos* Christology" in order to affirm a kind of universal Christ or a "Universal Presence" of Christ in the world. We would have recognized that Jesus, resurrected from the dead and living today as a person, though now noncorporeal, is actually "present" as a person—not as a vague impersonal "*logos*" or "spirit"—everywhere in the world. Freed of space and time limitations, he is "present" in the same way that God is present as Father, Son, and Holy Spirit. Later in this chapter I will deal with the way in which a Person Christology might shed light on the issue of the human and the divine in Jesus Christ and also on the mystery of the Trinity.

The point which I am making here is that if we take the resurrection seriously, we will understand it to mean that Jesus is a living person present today in the world as a person, not as a vague impersonal spirit or "*logos*." In fact, the "*logos*" concept as a "universal spirit" if viewed ontologically, is actually the antithesis of the concept of the individual person, Jesus Christ, risen and living today in person. The absolute idealism of Hegel has no place for the individual. It swallows up the individual soul in a kind of "world soul" or "absolute spirit." I am maintaining that this Hegelian idea of a universal spirit or a universal *logos* as an ontological category is pure fiction.

We may speak of a "universal spirit" in the sense of shared values, an esprit d' corps, or a universal "mood" such as the dream of world brotherhood or the longing for world peace. But such a universal spirit does not exist ontologically in and of itself. It is only a concept in the minds of individual persons. In a metaphysical sense such a spirit may be a reality as a rational or emotional feeling of human beings around the world. But it has no ontological reality in and of itself apart from the minds of persons who conceive it. So far as our personal experience goes, there are only two kinds of ontological reality: persons—self-conscious thinking, willing, self-transcending indivisible units of consciousness—and nonpersons, which we call things or objects. Jesus of Nazareth, Jesus Christ, was and is a person. He never was and is not today a spirit or a *logos* in the sense of a kind of impersonal force, or, as some would put it, a kind of "personal" force that is not a person—whatever that might mean. Jesus as a person may exert a force or an influence, and we may call this force or influence the *logos*, (Cobb: *Creative Transformation*) but he is not simply himself a force in the sense of a "power" or an "influence." If this latter were true, it would make him into an "it," a thing. Today philosophers sometimes refer to the person with the impersonal term subjectivity, but a person cannot be an *it*—a vague dispersed spirit or a "subjectivity." The term *locus* is of course a spatial term and can apply only analogically to a person who is noncorporeal. A thing has a locus, but a person does not, though in the case of a human person we may speak of the physical body as the locus of the person. A vague dispersed "spirit" is a "thing" not a "person," though it may be a function of a person or persons. Jesus, risen and living, cannot be reduced to simply a function (an *it*) of human or divine consciousness, which both Bultmann and the *Logos* Christology tend to do.

Note that John Cobb in developing his *Logos* Christology says, "Buddhism is chosen as a particularly important example of the kind of tradition in the face of which Christian theology should reconceive Christ."[27] This statement raises the question: "Is Christ who he is, Jesus Christ, a risen living person?" Or is he simply an object or a "thing" as we conceive and reconceive him to be? Is he simply a function of our consciousness? Clearly for Cobb, "Christ" is a concept of our minds, a principle and not Jesus Christ the living person. "Christ" is completely separated from Jesus of Nazareth and becomes simply a concept of Cobb's mind. He speaks of Christ as the "principle of creative transformation." Following this approach of severing all connection between Christ and the historical reality of Jesus of Nazareth, "Christ" can be made to mean anything the writer chooses, which is basically what Cobb does.

We reject this philosophical "*logos*" approach and insist that the Christian Faith is and must continue to be (if it is to remain the Christian Faith) rooted in the historical events of the first century. Any talk of "Christ" apart from being rooted in the life and person of Jesus of Nazareth becomes a philosophy or an ideology. We also reject the medieval philosophy of realism on which Cobb's *Logos* Christology is based, namely the view that universals are ontologically real. We are maintaining along with the medieval nominalists that universals may have a metaphysical reality in terms of ideas, concepts, human values, ideals, etc., but not an ontological reality in and of themselves. Ontologically, I repeat, we experience two types of reality: (1) persons, ourselves, and others (possibly also angels and demons) and God; and (2) things such as material objects as well as ideas, ideals, values, etc. of our own and of others' minds. Martin Buber speaks of this ontology in terms of the relationships which he calls "I–Thou" and "I–it." In other words, the only realities we experience are persons and things. What we call universals are things. They are simply concepts of human minds, values, ideals, thoughts, etc., including the metaphysical aspects of culture. They are functions of human minds or the Divine Mind. I do not question the importance of universals as concepts of persons, divine or human. Such concepts and ideals can and do have a powerful influence in human affairs and can be metaphysical realities which inspire or degrade or otherwise affect human life. But they have no ontological reality in and of themselves apart from the minds of the persons who conceive them and articulate them. As ontological realities in and of themselves they simply do not exist. All ontological reality that does not consist of a person or persons (human or divine) is nonperson or a thing or things, including ideas, universals, concepts, etc. To speak of Jesus Christ as a *logos* in the world or a universal spirit in the sense of an ontological reality is to reduce him to a thing. We insist that Jesus Christ was and is, and will forever remain a person, the divine–human person.

Metaphysics and Ontology

Our discussion of Person Christology has led us squarely into meta-physics and ontology: Some theologians in recent years have insisted that philosophy has no place in theological discussions. However, if the theologian speaks at all, he presupposes some form of metaphysics and some form of ontology, whether he recognizes it or not. Gerald O'Collins is correct when he says that "Kasper rightly requires that every Christology must be properly philosophical. Any serious discussion of Jesus Christ brings us into the deep water where we confront the final meaning of reality and the most basic needs of man. An undertow of philosophical issues tugs at Christology from start to finish."[28] It is not within our purview to go into technical philosophical issues related to the Incarnation. For that purpose, I refer the reader to such books as *The Logic of God Incarnate* by Thomas Morris referred to above. However, I do wish to make a proposal for better understanding of the Incarnation, which is the bedrock of the Christian faith.[29]

As we consider the ontology of Person Christology, I need, first, to distinguish between my use of *metaphysics* and my use of *ontology*. Some theologians and philosophers use the terms interchangeably, but we will distinguish between them. I use *ontology* to refer to the "being" or the "beingness" of persons and things. The ontology of something can be either physical, whatever science may determine this to be, or non-physical, as in the case of spiritual beings, ideas, ideals, concepts, etc., whereas *metaphysics* refers only to the non-physical or that which is "meta" or "above" or "beyond" the physical. Metaphysics I use to refer to non-physical qualities and values possessed by, expressed by, or ascribed to persons, either as individuals or groups. Qualities and values (or disvalues) such as truth, beauty, goodness, justice, love, hate, greed, spirit, esprit d' corps, etc. are not ontological realities in and of themselves. They are "secondary" realities in an ontological sense, dependent on the person or persons who think, love, hate, or hold values and concepts and/or express them in some way. I speak of these qualities, concepts, or values as meta-physical realities, but not ontological realities.

For the ontological materialist the only reality is matter. For the onto-logical idealist the only reality is mind or spirit. For the ontological dualist, reality is composed of both mind and matter. Below I am proposing a different kind of ontological dualism, not a dualism of mind and matter, but a dualism of person and nonperson. Ontological dualism has usually taken the Cartesian mind–body or spirit–matter form, positing two completely different kinds of reality, or as some would put it, two completely different "substances." Descartes, the seventeenth century philosopher, saw the two realities so totally different from each other as to make any contact or interaction between them impossible. Thus, the question became: How can the mind in any way affect the body and how can the body in any way affect the mind? Descartes precluded any interaction between the two, and allowed only what came to be known as parallelism. Thus the most extreme dualism is spoken of as Cartesian dualism.

In the history of philosophy, the concept of the person has been based at various times and by various thinkers on each of these three ontologies. The materialistic monist sees the person as a material object, a biological organism. What we think of as mind or spirit or soul, the materialist sees as simply the functioning of the biological organism, with the chief organ being the brain. Such materialists are spoken of as "physicalists" or, in psychological terms, "behaviorists." For them, the person is nothing more than a certain specie of living organism, a certain specie of animal.

In our modern scientific, secular age, the predominant view of scientists in the fields of physiology, psychology, and other disciplines that focus on the human being or the human person has become that of materialistic monism or physicalism. In the early 1950s, Gilbert Ryle, in his *The Concept of Mind*,[30] blasted Cartesian dualism in favor of a materialistic monism. The majority of contemporary students focusing on the study of the so-called "mind–body problem" have tended toward this emphasis on physicalism. For example, the recent book by Daniel Dennett, *Consciousness Explained*, seeks to explain the mind or the person as a physiological machine-like organism with the brain as the main source of what we speak of as "mind." In a recent feature article on the brain in *Newsweek* magazine, Dennett is quoted as saying that "the mind is somehow nothing but a physical phenomenon. In short, the mind is the brain."[31] When pushed, however, he admits that his scientific theories are tentative and concludes by saying, "and in a way it's a point of faith." Incidentally, we should not overlook Dennett's confirmation of what I say in chapter one concerning the inevitability of a faith stance or an unproven starting point for all of us.

At the other extreme, the idealistic monist sees the person as pure spirit or "mind." The body or the material aspects of human beings are not real in and of themselves, but are simply functions of or expressions of the non-material soul or mind. In what is called "absolute idealism" the individual person is seen as a specific expression of what is called "the absolute spirit" or "world soul." The individual person is "swallowed up" in "world soul" very much as a cup of ocean water is "swallowed up" when poured into the ocean, becoming a part of the ocean. In contrast, the view of "personal idealism" sees all reality as in some sense "personal," with every unit of reality being in some sense a "person." We will look at this position in more detail as we proceed. Idealistic monism, whether of the "absolute" or "personal" variety, has few exponents today.

The ontological dualist, believing that both spirit and matter are real, asserts that the person is made up of both. Some dualists think of the person as primarily the soul or the spirit or the mind that inhabits the body, though both are real. Others think of the person as a kind of equally balanced mind–body combination. Still others think of the person primarily as the physical organism or physical human being, the mind being simply a function of the physical organism. The first are dualists leaning toward idealism; the second are dualists trying to maintain a balance between mind and body; the third are dualists leaning toward physicalism. The most thorough and consistent dualists in this understanding of dualism are those for whom matter and spirit, though both a part of the person, are so totally different that there can be no interaction, only what is called parallelism. Yet, both mind and body make up the human being or "person." The human being is a thorough duality.

We obviously cannot go into all aspects of the ontology of persons or the full meaning of personhood. There are the biological, physiological, psychological, sociological, axialogical, and other aspects. To go into all of these would be far beyond the scope of this essay. For our purpose, it will be sufficient simply to define the term *person* as a being with self-awareness, self-transcendence, the ability to think both imaginatively and rationally, to set goals, and to carry out activities designed to reach those goals.[32] In what follows we will be dealing with this definition in more detail as we discuss the philosophy of personalism.

Likewise, the term *personalism* is used by philosophers in a number of different contexts and with a number of different shades of meaning. In some cases, it carries only the social and ethical implications of personhood, referring to the way persons conceive of themselves in relation to other persons and the world around them (self-identity), and to the way they comport themselves in relation to other persons (ethics). In this study we will take as axiomatic that personalism refers to those ethical norms and personal values that center around the highest moral and ethical concepts of human persons. However, our focus will not be at this point. Rather, we will focus on the ontology of persons in the sense of their "beingness." We will focus on the question: What is a person ontologically? Rejecting both idealistic monism and materialistic physicalism, as well as Cartesian mind–body dualism, we will seek to develop what we will call a dualistic ontology of "person and nonperson," which when we think seriously about reality, is what we actually experience in daily life.

Atomic and quantum physics make clear that no longer can the line be drawn between that which is "material" (hard stuff) and that which is "non-material" (soft stuff). Yet, we also reject both materialistic and idealistic monism. Reality is dualistic, but this is not a dualism of spirit and matter or mind and body. It is a dualism of persons and all that is not a person or persons. This is what we actually experience in everyday life. "Person" can be either human or divine, and at the human level can embrace both the material and the non-material or "spiritual." Though "person" per se is not physical, person at the human level involves and utilizes what we call the physical. At the divine level, "person" is pure spirit and completely non-material—certainly, in the sense that we ordinarily speak of the material, though this concept is constantly changing, and after all, God created the world, so cannot be totally unrelated. However, the essence and meaning of "person," as we will delineate below, is the same for both human and divine, though of course, the divine person and human person are quite different. "Nonperson" can be either material, as in the case of physical objects, or non-material, as in the case of ideas, concepts, ideals, values, etc., Thus, we see that the old ontological dichotomy of mind and body or spirit and matter is obliterated in favor of a new ontology. It is my contention that ontological reality is dual and that it falls into one of these two ultimate categories: persons and things. By "persons," as indicated above, I do not mean physical bodies, though bodies at the human level are obviously involved with persons. Bodies are things. Also, thoughts, ideas, ideals, etc., though functions of a person or persons, are things. At the human level, obviously, persons are involved with these "things," but "things" cannot be persons, and persons cannot be things. Let us now turn to an explication and development of this ontology.

To help clarify what we mean by the term *person* and by a *Person Christology* with the ontological concepts it involves in terms of the modern day use of the word person, we begin with a look at an approach to personalistic philosophy which developed in America in the late nineteenth and early twentieth centuries. This personalistic philosophy, which made an exhaustive attempt to define the modern concept of person, was developed primarily by Borden Parker Bowne, Albert C. Knudson, and Edgar Sheffield Brightman, professors at Boston University, hence the term "Boston Personalism."

Boston Personalism posits an ontological monism of "person." All reality is reducible to some form of "person." In other words, reality in the ultimate ontological sense is made up of persons. Bowne says, "This self-conscious existence [person] is the truly ultimate fact."[33] Though one finds a number of difficulties with this position, it is important to note that in the past fifty years, quantum physics with the principle of indeterminism and more of an open universe has moved in Bowne's direction. Scientists today do not know what matter is. Is it made up ultimately of particles, atoms, electrons, electromagnetic fields, wave lengths, energy, or something else? Maybe there is a sense in which at its deepest core, matter is similar to, or at least akin to person. Some philosophers are suggesting that modern physics demands a new metaphysics.[34] In terms of modern physics Bowne is not too far afield when he says, "Metaphysics shows that the fundamental reality must be conceived not as an extended stuff, but as an agent to which the notion of divisibility has no application."[35] The "process ontology" of Alfred North Whitehead seems to have some affinity to what Bowne is saying, though Whitehead's position is not easy to understand or categorize. It certainly is not a form of "personalism." Increasingly scientists are finding themselves describing ultimate reality in terms of symbols that are closer to the spiritual or non-material than they are to what we think of as material reality.

This view of Bowne that everything that exists is a person must be examined, particularly in the light of these developments in modern physics. What is it to be a person, not merely in a psychological or social sense, but in an ontological sense?[36] This is not an easy question to answer. We are forced to use empirical language—if we are to communicate at all—to describe a nonempirical reality, and this in the strict sense is doomed to failure from the beginning. We cannot describe the nonempirical with empirical language. We can only use analogy and metaphor. The best we can do is to "point toward" by means of analogy and hope that we communicate meaning and that the concept becomes clear or at least understandable.

Edgar Sheffield Brightman, a disciple of Bowne, says, "Personality [is] a conscious unity of self-experience,"[37] and "a person, then, is a conscious or spiritual unity."[38] When a personalist speaks of a self or person, he means "a conscious unity."[39] A person, then, is a specific being who has these qualities: consciousness, self-awareness, unity, undividedness, wholeness, self-identity, self-transcendence, and "think-ability" in the sense of both rational and imaginative thought. A person cannot be a component of something else and hence cannot be a substance or a particle which goes to make up some other thing. Neither can a person be a composite made up of parts. A person is an indivisible unity.

Yet, as we look at both Bowne and Brightman we discover serious inconsistencies. With all of the clear emphasis on the unity, the indivisibility, the self-awareness, the rational consciousness of the basic irreducible unit of reality, the person, both Bowne and Brightman in a way that is quite inconsistent, go on to talk about nonconscious, nonaware, nonfeeling, nonsensing, nonremembering, nondesiring, nonwilling, divisible entities as being in some sense personal or person. The term *person* is seemingly made to stretch over both conscious and nonconscious reality. Somehow all reality is personal whether conscious or not. Brightman says, "The personalistic theory of substance may be summarized in the words, 'substance is person.'"[40]

For Bowne there seem to be different levels of "personal" being, some conscious, some unconscious. Brightman makes a distinction between the "self" and the "person." A "person" is a "self" that has come to the level of rational thought. In Brightman's view, everything that exists is a "self." Yet he says, "What seems not to be a self is part of or aspect or experience of a self or selves."[41] Which does Brightman hold? Is everything a self, a "unity of consciousness," or are some things "a part of or aspect or experience of a self or selves"? A self has been defined as an indivisible unit, yet here it is divisible into "parts" or "aspects." How can an "indivisible, irreducible unity of varied consciousness" be divided into parts? Likewise, when we are talking about "a part" or "an aspect" we are talking about a thing. Is a person a thing? Further inconsistency is seen in Brightman's statement, "Nothing exists except in, of, and for a self." Is "everything real a self?" Or do some things exist for selves? We cannot have it both ways. Either all reality, every individual unit however small, is a person, or a self, a thinking, self-transcending indivisible unit of consciousness which is what Bowne and Brightman seemingly contend, or else some reality is not a person or a self, but part of a person or self, or exists for a person or self. Since a person is an indivisible unity, how can a person have parts or aspects? An ontology which affirms not a monism of person, but an ontological dualism composed of persons *and* that which is not a person seems to fit better both the empirical facts we experience and also rational thought. The category of nonperson would include material things, ideas, and concepts, and what Brightman speaks of as the less than rational "self." There is a clear ontological distinction between a person (thinking, self-transcending, purposing, willing, setting goals, etc.) and nonperson (minus all these attributes). Yet the old mind–body, spirit–matter dualism has been erased by modern physics.

The inconsistency involved in Bowne's and Brightman's position appears to grow out of their attempt to force everything into a monistic ontology. If, as Brightman says, a person is a "unity of consciousness," I see no way for a piece of wood, or its component elements, atoms, or smaller particles (or whatever atoms are made of) to be a person or "personal." Personal is an adjective and when used properly, refers to the attributes of a person. If used as a noun or an hypostatization,[42] it appears to say something, but actually says nothing. When Brightman says, "a personalist is one who holds that everything real is a self at some level of its existence," the contradiction in speaking of a self as an "it" is apparent. "It" refers to impersonal reality.

This same kind of inconsistency is found in those, such as Paul Tillich, who speak of ultimate reality, "Being itself," (note the "it"), as in some sense "personal" but not a person. Of course the reason, as explained by John Hick, quoted above, is that the term *person* seems too anthropomorphic. However, is it any more anthropomorphic than "personal?" Since "person" is defined in nonmaterial terms, a person is not inherently human in the sense of being necessarily dependent on the mortal or physical body. Therefore, while the term *person* for God may conjure up the imagery of an old man with a long white beard somewhere in the sky, it does not of necessity carry such anthropomorphic connotations. In fact, in both theology and philosophy, the term *person* for God carries a quite different meaning, and this is generally understood.

Those who reject the use of the term *person* for God are caught in the dilemma of having to use the pronoun "it" for that reality to which they are ascribing qualities and actions which are only properly applied to a person, a "her" or a "him." Unfortunately the English language does not have a personal pronoun for the third person singular that implies neither male nor female. The pronoun "it" is third person, but is impersonal. An existentialist philosopher says, "Being takes the initiative in addressing man, in giving him speech, in setting him in the light and openness. Being is gracious toward man and constitutes him *its* guardian." [Italics mine.] Here we have six action verbs with personal action initiated and carried out by an "it." "Its"—that is, trees, mountains, stars, the universe, space, even "ultimate reality," etc.—are not initiators of personal, purposive action such as grace. They do not "take initiative," "address," "give him speech," "set him in the light," "constitute him its guardian." We are in a hopeless confusion of thought to speak of an "it," even if it is a universal "it," as doing things that only a person, either human or divine, can do. Note that in referring to "man" (a personal being) the writer uses the pronoun, "him."[43]

We therefore reject the ontological monism proposed by Bowne and suggest the ontological dualism of "person" and "nonperson" delineated above. Possibly a better terminology for what I am proposing might be "person and *preperson*," which may be more adequate to describe the ontological reality we experience in both the empirical and the nonempirical world around us. I believe "nonperson" or what is commonly called "matter" is a reality, and is not "person." However, it is not alien to person, for it has the potential for becoming person, as when it is taken up through metabolism or the birth process or by other means and is appropriated by or becomes a person. But whether we use the term nonperson or preperson, the meaning is the same. There likely are a number of ways that preperson (or nonperson) may become a person. Preperson is not person, for preperson is an "it," a "thing," or "things," as for example, the human egg cell, which, when fertilized, can become a person. "Person" cannot be preperson, for a person is a unique and distinct, unitary, self-conscious reality, an "I" or "Thou," never an "It," and therefore cannot be made up of parts, as can preperson or nonperson. If we are to be strictly accurate we cannot speak of "person," but must always speak of a person or persons, for all persons are unitary and distinct, each a "locus" or "center" of self-consciousness. Therefore, the term "personal" cannot be properly used as a noun substitute for the person himself or herself. The proper use of the term *personal* is as a description of the qualities that make up a person. A thing can never be a person. A person can never be a thing, though a person may be treated by another person as a thing, as Buber points out. But preperson can become person, as when a human egg cell, an "it," a "thing," is fertilized and in time becomes a person. The center of the abortion debate is the question: When or at what point does an "it" become a "he" or a "she"? This clearly indicates the kinship of person and nonperson, and is the reason the term "preperson" rather than "nonperson," can in some situations be more accurate, though either term is acceptable.

Bowne seems to agree basically with what I am saying here so long as he does not try to force an ontological monism of person. He defines person in this way: "The essential meaning of personality is selfhood, self consciousness, self-control, and the power to know. . . . Any being, finite or infinite, which has knowledge and self-consciousness and self-control is personal; for the term has no other meaning."[44] Further, he maintains that the person is nonmaterial and noncorporeal, though corporeality may be a mode of expression of a person: "Man himself in his essential personality is as unpicturable and formless as God."[45] And this is true, Bowne says, "not merely in the sense of not lying within the sphere of visibility in any way. . . . Indeed, the most familiar events of every day life have their key and meaning only in the invisible."[46]

Bowne says, "The physical organism is only an instrument for expressing and manifesting the inner life, but the living self is never seen."[47] Einstein declared, ". . . time and space are modes by which we think and not conditions in which we live."[48] Thus the real person, the real "I" is not limited by time and space. I can live in the past; I can live in the present; I can live in the future; or I can live timelessly where I experience eternal values, though my experience is itself at present in time. These qualities of a person, we might point out here, make possible the Incarnation and the Trinitarian understanding of God, as will be indicated below.

Bowne points to the familiar fact that a camera recording moving persons on a street would see only objects similar to moving balls on a billiard table. The "persons" are not visible for they are not the physical objects moving up and down the street, but the invisible wills, the invisible "centers" of self-conscious decision making. The camera only records physical movements which apart from some interpretation not apparent in the pictures at all, are meaningless "atoms in motion." We can only assume that the moving objects are directed by some inner unseen and unseeable motivation. But nothing in the pictures themselves, that is, in the physiological, observable aspects of the objects shows this in any way. We can only infer by our own imagination that various "purposes" are the cause of the movements, that is, one is on her way to her office, one is going shopping, and another is headed home. The persons are invisible.

Bowne asserts, "Personality and corporeality are incommensurable ideas."[49] I would not go this far, for I believe persons and corporeality are definitely related as far as human beings are concerned, and as Christians we believe God created the world. However, what Bowne is asserting I do agree with, namely that "persons" are conscious, thinking, centers of self-awareness, whereas "corporeality" is nonthinking, nonconscious reality. However, the dividing line is not between "mind" and "matter," but between "person" (self-conscious, thinking reality) and "nonperson" (that which is not self-conscious, thinking reality). This is what I call an ontological dualism of person and nonperson. If this is what Bowne means, I agree. However, I would insist that the two, far from being "incommensurable" are, though distinctly different, yet compatible. They are not antithetical. Nonperson can and does become "person," as in the birth of a child. Whether a person (not his body, which is already nonperson) can regress to nonperson is not clear. It would be possible for this to happen in death, assuming the Hebrew concept of man as a psycho-physical unity. Death would be the movement from person to nonperson, and Resurrection would be the "recreation" from nonperson into person or the raising again of the person in a "form" different from that which in the present world is in the corporeal body. However this may be, Bowne contends that human or physical limitations (time and space) are not a necessary part of the notion of person or personhood: "Fullness of power, knowledge, and selfhood which alone are essential factors of the conception of personality are not corporeally based."[50]

Before closing this chapter I wish to deal with the implications of Person Christology for the "two-natures" and trinitarian controversies. The issues of classical Christology, faced in the early church councils, centered around both the nature and the work of Christ. The crucial question was: "How can we, if we can, affirm that Jesus Christ was both fully human and fully divine?" Greek and Latin philosophical terminology including such words as "substance," "nature," "person," etc. were used in an attempt to state in terms of a dialectic what the church fathers sensed as true but which defied any kind of logical formulation. Those theologians such as Sabellius, Arius, Apollanarius, Nestorius, and others who came out with what seemed to be a logical and rational statement of the two natures of Christ were in time declared heretical. We as Christians have come to see that in the

Incarnation we have a mystery which we believe is true, but which defies all human attempts to formulate in a strictly logical and rational way.

With this in mind I want to suggest that while we make no claim to solve the mystery, we do believe that the insights of a "Person Christology" may shed some light and may aid in our approach to the mystery. As indicated above, a "person" is not bound by space and time. Through self-transcendence, a person combines, and in a sense erases, the distinction in past, present, and future. Though human persons, as presently embodied in space and limited by time, are bound by these factors, a person *per se*, human or divine, is not material, and thus is not so bound inherently. There is, therefore, no logical contradiction in holding that a given person is *per se* both a human person from a human perspective, and at the same time the divine person from the divine perspective. This is, up to a point, what is affirmed as the identity of God and man in some Eastern religions. Only when we get into stating attributes of the divine and the human person do we run into contradictions, and we should remember that these attributes are always stated from a human perspective.

One may want to ask why, then, in this sense could not every person be both divine and human, as the Indian Vedanta and some other Eastern philosophies hold? Likewise, some Christian theologians assert that there is a "spark" of the divine (the *Logos*) in every person. The answer is that though the nature of person or personhood clearly makes this possible (and in Jesus it is actual), God has also willed human freedom. I am not suggesting that the divine–human Jesus was not free, only that human freedom has been exercised by the rest of humanity against God and not in harmony with God's will, which was not the case with Jesus; so this identification is not automatic. Human sin, human rebellion come in. In the biblical view, though created in the image of God, man clearly is a creature and through rebellion becomes a "fallen" sinful creature far from identical with God. Nothing could be clearer in the biblical understanding of man, and it is at this point that the biblical view is the exact opposite of Eastern views such as the Vedanta. This biblical view is the basis of the clear distinction between Jesus Christ, the God–man, and other human beings. We have seen that for John Cobb the distinction between Jesus Christ and other human beings is a matter of degree. Christ simply has more of the *Logos*, which is in lesser degree in all persons, and indeed in all things. Cobb's view has some interesting similarities to Indian Vedanta which declares that "Atman is Brahman" (the "spirit" or essence of man is the same as that of God except in lesser degree). In the Person Christology I am proposing, there is a clear distinction between God and man. The God–man, Jesus Christ, is both human and divine by the will of God. The Supreme Person, God, by his own will expresses himself corporeally through the Incarnation and thus limits himself, becoming flesh in Jesus Christ. Nevertheless, by the same will and act of God, the divine–human person, Jesus Christ, is also God. This view is thoroughly consistent with the concept of person as defined above. It is also consistent with the biblical understanding of God and man.

At least a part of the problem of the ancient fathers was that they operated with an inadequate concept of both God and man. They thought in Platonic terms of two totally disparate and incompatible realms—the realm of "ideas" or "ideal forms" and the realm of "shadows" or the "unreal." They saw God too much in Platonic terms as totally transcendent and far away, a "totally other," to use Karl Barth's phrase. They understood man to be basically "flesh" or animal, a totally different "substance" from God. How could these two totally different and completely incompatible "substances" be united in one? They did not take the biblical language "in the image of God created he them" with sufficient seriousness. While, as we have just asserted, the biblical view certainly does not identify humanity with God, as is done in the Indian Vedanta, humanity is in God's image, and a persistent strain of Christian theology has maintained that Jesus Christ in the flesh was not only fully God, but was also fully human as humanity was created to be, that is, perfect humanity. Therefore, the human, while in no sense identical with the divine, is likewise, as created, not incompatible with the divine, and in the sense just stated, the human person and the divine person were by the will of God one person (in the modern sense of person) in Jesus Christ—the divine–human person.

Returning to pluralism and the relationship to other religions, we hold that this is the real uniqueness in the Christian faith. Christianity as a religion is certainly not unique. The real uniqueness is in Jesus Christ: He was God in human flesh, (in "time" and "space" categories), born in a stable, growing to manhood, crucified, dead, buried, and risen. He is God in the person of the risen and living Jesus. He will be God (from the human perspective of time) in a timeless future. His resurrection demonstrates that he is God in person— the Divine-Human Person existing noncorporeally in the world. This is his uniqueness. He is different from all human persons who ever lived, who live today, and who will ever live in the future, in that he is God. God chose—

willed to become a human person—Jesus Christ, while at the same time remaining (in space-time categories) the Supreme Person, God. He was and is at the same time (in space-time categories) the divine–human person, Jesus Christ, and also God, the Father, Creator of heaven and earth.

In terms of pluralism, this way of explaining the divine–human in Jesus Christ will raise again for many the specter of the pre-1900 truth–falsehood dichotomy and the unholy attitude of Christians toward non-Christians. I am extremely sensitive to the evils in the superiority claim, as I have made clear above, and I reject it completely. But I would remind the reader first that we are speaking of a person accessible to all people, not of an institution, the church, or Christianity, a religion. It is true that Jesus Christ happens to be the fountainhead of a historic religion, Christianity, that at times has been dogmatic, arrogant, and un-Christian in attitudes and actions. For this we can only repent. Second, I would remind the reader that we testify to a belief we have found true in experience and seek a rational understanding of our experience. We do not argue. Others may experience something quite different and this we not only respect, but honor, though we may disagree. We will say more about this matter momentarily. We must stress that we are not speaking about institutions, or "religions," or movements, or religious communities. We are not making claims about Jesus, and we refuse to do so, though we recognize that our experience and the belief based on that experience make a clear assumption as to who he was and is. We are only testifying to an experience, and trying to understand that experience. With Anselm, our goal is faith seeking understanding—not argument. Indeed, as we will see in chapter four, the issue of salvation, cast not in the old "exclusivistic" terms, but in dynamic personal terms, is the crucial place where Person Christology has the most to say. Traditional Christian soteriology has been seen too much in static, forensic, institutional terms rather than in dynamic personal terms, and it is here that unholy claims to exclusivism, superiority, finality, have arisen. It is noteworthy that this static view of salvation appears to be the presupposition of most of those who have trouble with the uniqueness of Jesus Christ and thus insist that we must give up Christian uniqueness and "cross the Rubicon" to complete relativism. They thus insist that salvation as they understand it is available in all religions. What they seem not to realize is that they have a truncated view of salvation and that where salvation is available depends in no small measure on our definition and understanding of salvation, to which we now turn in the next chapter.

Chapter Four
OFFER THEM CHRIST

THE SAVIOR

IN CHAPTERS ONE, TWO, AND THREE WE HAVE FOCUSED ON Christology, on Jesus Christ as the Absolute, the Way, the Truth, and the Life. This is at the center of the Christian faith, the world mission of the church, and the relationship of the Christian faith to other religions. We have developed what we are calling a Person Christology, stressing that Jesus Christ is a living person today—the divine–human person, who is the Way, the Truth, and the Life. In this chapter we turn our attention to this Jesus as the Savior of humankind.

In dealing with the question of salvation, we need first to be sure that we are clear what we mean by the term. In the modern world, even within Christian circles, it is used in different ways. If we should include other religious traditions, the variety of meanings would be considerably increased and in some cases the adherents of those religions would not know what we were talking about. *Salvation* is clearly a western term. It is not even clear if the word has any valid place in some of the religious traditions of the world, or if it can be validly used in these traditions. Chester Gillis points out in regard to Buddhism: "As with Hinduism, and probably more so, the use of the term *salvation* is inappropriate. Buddhists neither aspire to salvation in the Western sense, nor are they saved by any external divine force or intervention."[1] So salvation in the Christian sense carries a special meaning.

That we are saved through faith in Jesus Christ is the most basic belief of Christians. That Jesus' death on the cross was a sacrifice for our sins and the source of our salvation, was proclaimed from the earliest days by Saint

Paul and the first Christians. Over time there developed a number of different ways of understanding and describing what Jesus accomplished through his death on the cross. As Christian theology developed, a number of theories and various terminology to express them emerged, all of which were related in one way or another to life in the Roman Empire of the first and second centuries. Some of these theories or paradigms are:

Atonement: This term is taken from the cultic temple sacrificial system of the day. Christ becomes the sacrifice offered as an atonement for our sin.

Ransom, Redemption: These terms come from the marketplace where slaves were bought and sold. Christ "redeems" the sinner who is a "slave" to sin and to Satan. Christ pays the ransom and sets the slave free.

Justification: This term is derived from the law court. The purpose of the defense is to justify the accused. In God's court the human being stands condemned because he/she is a sinner. There is no way to plead innocent. We know and God knows that we are guilty. Only the forgiving grace of God can save us. Through Jesus' death on the cross and our faith in Christ, God declares us "just and righteous," even though we remain always sinners saved by grace.

Substitution: We are guilty of rebellion, of sin, of transgressing God's law. We deserve to die. The penalty cannot be escaped. In order to maintain a just universe the penalty (death) must be carried out. So Christ becomes the substitute, suffering death in the place of the sinner.

Liberation: This term is taken from the context of the Roman prison. Because of sin we are imprisoned by Satan. Christ liberates us from prison.

Reconciliation: This term is taken from the context of revolt, rebellion, and estrangement. Because of rebellion against God we are estranged from him. Christ, the mediator, reconciles us to God and God to us.

Conquering: Christ conquers sin. This term is taken from the battlefield. What Christ does is to conquer Satan and the forces of evil, the demonic powers. We can thus be victorious. This is the *Christus Victor* concept in which through his death, Christ storms the gates of hell, Satan's headquarters, and conquers Satan. It is reflected in the version of the Apostles' Creed which includes the phrase, "He descended into hell."

Each of these paradigms expresses a meaningful aspect of salvation in the truly Christian sense. They are all valid. Salvation for most persons, generally speaking, has usually referred simply to being saved to go to heaven. One finds that this is still the basic meaning in the discussions concerning Christianity and other religions. It is certainly the meaning assumed by those who hold to Christian "exclusivism" or "inclusivism" as well as by those who attack these positions. It is the meaning assumed by Karl Rahner's "Anonymous Christian" approach and also by Hans Kung's delineation of other religions as "ordinary means of salvation." The recent books, *No Other Name?*, *The Myth of Christian Uniqueness*, and *A Universal Theology of Religion*, cited above, also presuppose this "other worldly" usage of the word salvation. Though this is obviously an extremely important aspect of *salvation* (all of us want to go to heaven when we die), it is not the only meaning of salvation in the Christian sense of the word. We need to be aware of this fact and make clear what we mean when we speak of salvation. As always, the answer to a question depends in no small measure on precisely what the question is asking. In Christian theology the term has always carried the connotation of present well-being in addition to its eschatological meaning. Today in certain theological circles the word has also acquired both economic and political connotations. The Hebrew roots out of which the word *salvation* comes carry the connotation of total "well-being" for the individual, or deliverance of the whole nation from oppression or from some other evil. The Hebrews did not separate the physical and the spiritual as we, following Greek philosophical dualism, often do today. Taking a cue from this Old Testament understanding, a strand of contemporary theology has developed a view of salvation which places as much stress on the physical as on the spiritual, on the present age as on the age to come. Salvation in this sense his strong economic and political overtones as was clearly seen in the World Council of Churches Conference on "Salvation Today" in Bangkok in 1973

Salvation seen in political and economic terms takes its cue from the Exodus as deliverance from slavery and oppression. The massive upheavals in our day, the unparalleled economic and political oppressions and denials of simple justice, the rampant racism, sexism, and other affronts to human dignity so common today have given rise to what is being called "liberation theology." In this theology the term salvation takes on an almost exclusively secular or this-worldly meaning. Salvation in the traditional sense of being saved to go to heaven is not denied, but is very largely ignored. From a truly Christian perspective this understanding of salvation is obviously flawed, and though we certainly favor and work for the liberation of all peoples from all kinds of oppression and injustice, we insist that such liberation is not the full meaning of Christian salvation. Our question, then, is: What is a truly adequate understanding of Christian salvation? Another way of stating the question is: What is the whole gospel for the whole person for the whole world?

What I propose to do in this chapter is to examine the concept of salvation in the context of the Person Christology proposed in the previous chapters, and to suggest a model of salvation that includes both this worldly and otherworldly dimensions, truly the whole gospel for the whole person for the whole world. We call this a "Person Christology" because we focus on the person, Jesus Christ, risen from the grave and living today as a person, a real person whom we can meet and relate to in interpersonal encounter the same way that we can with any living person. What we also stress is that the nature of the living person, Jesus Christ, is such that an interpersonal encounter with him is always a life-changing experience and that this life-changing encounter is what we call "salvation." In order to make clear what we mean by salvation in this sense, I want to add another paradigm to the seven listed above. It is the paradigm of "Transformation" based on interpersonal encounter which I suggest in addition to the "Justification," "Reconciliation," etc., paradigms.

In chapter three we talked about the mystery of personhood and showed how even in everyday life one person can have a tremendously powerful and formative influence on another person simply through the force of the interpersonal encounter (best examples: mother-child, husband-wife). This is a fact which has been true and has been recognized from the beginning of history. However, in the twentieth century this interpersonal dynamic has become the subject of extensive study and research, and has come to be known as the discipline of psychology and psychotherapy. I want to suggest a paradigm from this discipline, but want to be very sure to make clear that I am not proposing a psychological approach to, or a psychological theory of salvation, as some have done. I will use the findings of the science of inter-personal dynamics, particularly psychotherapy or counseling therapy as a paradigm, but as a paradigm only. I have no expertise in psychology or coun-seling and am not proposing any kind of psychological theory of salvation. What I am doing is simply utilizing the findings of this study as a paradigm in order to point toward the way the divine–human person, Jesus Christ, may impact and transform our lives, which is what we mean by salvation.

For a long time, as the science of counseling therapy developed, the approach used and the techniques applied by the therapist were considered the important thing which brought about the change or the healing in the person being counseled. In the last few years, however, we have come to see that this is not the case. A study done a few years ago by Charles E. Truax and Robert R. Carkhuff[2] concluded that the healing or recovery of a patient in counseling therapy is increasingly being seen not as an objective, some-thing which happens to the client as a result of certain "insights" the client gets or certain techniques that are applied. Rather it is the result of the inter-personal encounter, person to person, with the stability and quality of the personhood of the therapist as the key factor. The person being counseled is helped if and only if the counselor has certain qualities in order to be effec-tive. These qualities are:

Genuineness

The counselor must be authentic. He/she must be honest and sincere. Nothing comes through to the client in a counseling situation quicker than a phony counselor. The Truax-Carkhuff study stressed that "[for] the therapist within the relationship [to] be himself integrated, genuine and authentic seems most basic to the therapeutic outcome."[3] A person for whom counseling is a profession and not a calling, a job and not a voca-tion to which he/she is dedicated, comes through to the counselee as insincere. The therapist's role-playing and his professionalism will be sensed by the client and though the client may not know what the real problem is, any significant help in the counseling situation will be blocked. The study says: "Unless the parent or teacher is genuine in relating to the child, his warmth, caring and understanding have no meaning."[4] Further, the study points out that, "we [counselors] should aim at being what we are in our encounter—that we would openly be the feelings and attitudes that we are experiencing . . . coming into direct personal encounter with a child or patient or a spouse—a meeting on a person-to-person basis, which is often too rare."[5]

Maturity and Integration

If the counselor has hang-ups of his own which he has not resolved or has not come to terms with, they will be reflected in his counseling. If this happens to be the case with a given counselor, a number of possibilities are open to him/her. She/he may go through counseling herself/himself; sometimes psychoanalysis or other means of getting at what might be called a "hidden agenda" in the counselor may be of help. In whatever way it may be done, the counselor must deal with his/her own immaturities if he/she is to be effective. Maturity is a quality that comes from many sources. In whatever way it is gained, it is an absolute essential for an effective counselor.

Empathy

There must be more than integrity and maturity. The counselor must "be with" the person. The study emphasizes that, "to be facilitative toward another human being requires us to be deeply sensitive to the moment-to-moment 'being' of the other person and to grasp both the meaning and significance and the content of his experiences and feelings."[6] This "being with" the patient is crucial if the counselor is to aid in the healing process. The study states that

> The central ingredient of the psychotherapeutic process appears to be the therapist's ability to perceive and communicate accurately and with sensitivity the feelings of the patient and the meaning of those feelings. By communicating "I am with you" and "I can accurately sense the world as you construe it," in a manner that fully acknowledges feelings and experiences, he facilitates the patient's movement toward a deeper self-awareness and knowledge of his own feelings and experiences and their import.[7]

Scott Peck says, "It is almost impossible for a patient to experience significant personality growth without a 'therapeutic alliance' with the therapist. In other words, before the patient can risk major change he or she must feel the strength and security that come from believing that the therapist is the patient's constant and stable ally."[8]

Acceptance

The counselor must be able to listen to the patient without a judgmental attitude and with total acceptance of the person. This in no sense means condoning whatever the person may have done that is wrong. But it does mean that the person must feel totally accepted in spite of his/her wrongdoing. The counselor must focus on the person as a person—as a person of worth who is valued. The Truax-Carkhuff study stresses that to be helpful to another person "requires that we, at least to a certain high degree, accept and nonpossessively prize this other person."[9] This means that therapists must be "listeners as well as talkers" and cultivate "an ability to perceive sensitively and accurately the feelings and experiences and their meanings to another person."[10] Also, the counselor must be able to "communicate . . . this understanding in a language consistent with [the patient's] language."[11]

Non-Possessive Warmth

The client needs not only to feel that she/he is accepted as a person for what she/he is. She/he must feel a positive warmth. The adequate counselor will radiate to the patient a warmth which communicates at a deep visceral level: "I care for you; you are important to me; in short, I love you." But this love must be a totally nonpossessive love. To use the Greek terms, it must be *agape* love. Any element of *eros* love (possessive love) will skew and destroy the healing relationship, as many counselors with a Freudian orientation have discovered.[12] The person must be valued as a person, and this nonpossessive warmth must be communicated in such a genuine way that it is experienced by the person as such. The Truax-Carkhuff study found that "the ideal counselor or therapist would indeed provide . . . empathy, nonpossessive warmth and genuineness to all clients."[13]

Positive Reinforcement

Positive, outgoing, nonpossessive love and warmth in themselves will give to the patient a certain amount of positive reinforcement. However, the counselor must go beyond this in the sense of consciously reinforcing the positive, constructive elements which he/she senses in the person. This, again, must be genuine. It cannot be a false "bucking up" of the patient. It cannot be a shallow "cheer up, old fellow, everything is going to be all right," kind of thing. Rather, the therapist must be genuine in communicating: "You are a person of worth. With all of your faults and with all of the problems which we in no way gloss over, you have positive, constructive things going for you and you need to build on these." Such an attitude can enable the patient to engage in positive self-evaluation and can start a process which will reverse the negative, self-destructive attitudes that have been in control. Positive reinforcement is one of the major aims of therapy. The Truax-Carkhuff study found that "therapists or counselors who are high in empathy, warmth and genuineness are more effective in psychotherapy because they themselves are personally more potent positive reinforcers."[14] Also, such a therapist "increases the level of the patient's positive self-reinforcement."[15]

Finding Meaning

Seventh, the counselor must be able to assist the person in finding meaning. Through all of the above, the counselor will be an enabling agent helping the person to find meaning in his/her life. A sense of meaninglessness is the most destructive force in human personality. In a real sense the ultimate goal of therapy is the finding of meaning. This is true both at the human, psychotherapeutic level, and also at the divine or theological level where eternal salvation is the concern. An adequate therapist is one who can creatively assist in this process.

Stability

The eighth quality needed by a counselor is stability and firmness. Warmth and love must not be mistaken for softness and indulgence, else the entire therapeutic relationship is skewed and the results will be negative. The relationship of empathy with its contagious warmth is not to be a kind of "grandfatherly indulgence" or what Dietrich Bonhoefer called "cheap grace." It is firm and demanding as well as loving. Ruth Monroe points that out in the Adlerian approach,

> The therapist must temper his warmth and encouragement
> with understanding of the special problems of the patient, and

must bring the patient to the same understanding. . . . I use this
example to show that Adler's emphasis on warmth and encouragement was no namby-pamby "bucking up" treatment.[16]

The findings of the Truax–Carkhuff study concerning the ideal counselor or therapist might be summarized as follows: The therapist must be
one who is genuine, mature, integrated, honest, sincere, and authentic, who
possesses the ability to show empathy, acceptance, and a nonpossessive
warmth. He/she must be one who is able to give positive reinforcement
and to assist the client in finding meaning in life. He/she must be a strong,
positive person who possesses unwavering stability.

JESUS, THE WONDERFUL COUNSELOR

Now what does all of this have to do with Christology and Christian
salvation? Why have I gone into the therapeutic process, and particularly
the qualities of an effective counselor, in such depth? The answer is that I
am setting up a clear empirical paradigm. The central, all-important place
of the quality of personhood of the counselor in successful human therapy
is a paradigm that underscores forcefully the place of Jesus Christ, the
divine–human person in eternal salvation. An actual life-transforming
encounter with him is essential if we are to be cleansed, transformed, and
made whole. It is Jesus and Jesus only who has every quality of the
"Wonderful Counselor." Isaiah speaks of the Messiah as the "Wonderful
Counselor, Mighty God, Everlasting Father, the Prince of Peace" (Isa. 9:6)
who brings joy and peace to us. He is genuine, mature, integrated, has real
empathy for me, the sinner, gives genuine love, nonpossessive warmth, and
more. Yet, he is unwavering and firm in the demand that change (repentance) is absolutely essential.

Remember that the same ills, hurts, guilts, failures, and frustrations that
come into the psychotherapist's office come to the confessional, the prayer
meeting, the Bible study, and the mourner's bench. For life is all of one
piece. The only permanent and eternal healing is through the "Wonderful
Counselor," the divine–human person, Jesus Christ. Whenever the human
counselor is fortunate enough to be successful in dealing with some of
these ills, he/she is simply discovering more and more of the way God has
made human existence to work. In Colossians 1:16–17 Paul says, "All

things were created through him [Christ] and for him . . . and in him all things hold together." The Today's English Version puts it: "in union with him all things have their proper place." In the words of Lesslie Newbigin (quoted above), he is "the one who can make sense of the whole human situation which my partner and I share as fellow human beings."

E. B. Green in his study *The Meaning of Salvation* comments, "Guilt, moral defeat, loneliness, anxiety, the quest for meaning in life, death and beyond—these are still foes which plague the human spirit."[17] The quest for salvation involves the desire to deal effectively with these issues in life. It is my thesis that such deep problems of the human spirit as guilt, moral defeat, loneliness, anxiety, fear, anger, and a sense of meaninglessness only find solution, and the person experiencing them only finds salvation in an interpersonal relationship—in a saving, transforming encounter with a totally adequate person, and this person is Jesus Christ. It is well documented that the most formative factors in any person's life are the interpersonal relationships which he/she experiences. In fact, there is no such thing as change in one's personal life apart from an interpersonal relationship that has spawned it. There is first the interpersonal relationship with the mother, then the father, then siblings, and others. These relationships go far toward making the person what he/she is. The interpersonal relationship with Jesus Christ can indeed be the most formative of all. Jesus Christ is indeed the "Wonderful Counselor," the Savior. This is the essence of Person Christology. Jesus Christ, a living person, meets me today and in relationship—a deep "I–Thou" encounter, I am liberated, redeemed, set free, made whole. I am saved. I am now ready for eternity both this side and the other side of the grave.

Jesus in his earthly life and relationships with people as recorded in the pages of the New Testament, meets completely every qualification for an adequate counselor listed above. For example, when Truax and Carkhuff say, "By communicating 'I am with you' and 'I can accurately sense the world as you construe it' in a manner that fully acknowledges feelings and experiences, he facilitates the patient's movement toward a deeper self-awareness and knowledge of his own feelings and experiences and their import," they express what the New Testament expresses in the word "Immanuel," "I am with you." They state the true meaning of Incarnation. They also express in clinical terms what Paul means when he says, "Christ . . . lives in me . . . Who loved me and gave himself for me" (Gal. 2:20). Furthermore, the "pointing toward" of human psychotherapeutic experience goes further. Psychotherapists are beginning to discover that suffering is a necessary part of successful therapy. Scott Peck says, "As I look back on every successful case I have ever had I can see that at some point or points in each case I had to lay myself on the line. The willingness of the therapist to suffer at such moments is perhaps the essence of therapy, and when perceived by the patient, as it usually is, it is always therapeutic."[18]

The Christian gospel has always proclaimed this necessity of suffering. Jesus gave himself on the cross, suffered, and died for our salvation. The key is love: "God so loved the world." Jesus is therefore the "Wonderful Counselor," the one who "lays himself on the line," who loves to the uttermost, and suffers both with and for the counselee—the sinner. The qualities of a good counselor described above can be summed up in one word—*Agape*. Such suffering love is "always therapeutic" when "perceived by the patient"—and this is without regard to race, national, or ethnic origin or religious affiliation. There is no contest of religions here. Religious affiliation does not matter. It is a relationship with a person, a relationship of trust and love. Isaac Watts proclaimed the experience of the "patient," the sinner, when he wrote:

> When I survey the wondrous cross
> On which the prince of glory died,
> My richest gain I count but loss,
> And pour contempt on all my pride.

This surrender, this brokenness is essential. To become a "patient" or a "counselee," one must go to the Counselor through surrender, repentance, and faith. He/she must go to the foot of the cross, which is by far the hardest part. One must come to the Counselor of his or her own free will, whether it be with a human therapist at a human level, or the divine–human Counselor, Jesus Christ. It must be a decision, a free choice. Whether with a human counselor or with the Wonderful Counselor, ". . . empathy, warmth and genuineness may be effective with clients who are ready to be helped but ineffective with the poor prognosis clients."[19] No counselor, even the divine–human Counselor, Jesus Christ, can help a person until the person wants to be helped and surrenders. The cross is at the center of the Christian faith as the means of God's salvation for all persons because it is here that Jesus surrendered himself, making possible our surrender at the foot of the cross. But it is not just the "Christian Faith" which is involved here. In fact, the principle of "redeeming love," as seen on the cross and discovered by Scott Peck, is not a "religious" concept at all. It is a fundamental principle of life as life was created by God. Love is a relational term and "redeeming love" is found in a relationship with a person, Jesus Christ. John 1:4 says, "In him is life" and Life should be spelled with a capital "L." Salvation is never found in a relationship with an institution or a movement. It is only found in relationship with a person, Jesus Christ.

The practice of counseling therapy thus provides an excellent paradigm at the human level for what in the Christian faith is called "salvation"—if by salvation we mean dynamic and not static salvation. David Roberts[20] uses these terms to distinguish genuine from bogus salvation. Genuine Christian salvation is always dynamic salvation, producing what Paul calls the "new Creation." Mary Magdalene, Zacchaeus, the woman at the well in Samaria, and many others experienced this salvation through a simple interpersonal encounter with Jesus Christ. There were no "religious" forms or ceremonies involved. No religion was joined. If we will examine the eight qualities of an effective psychotherapeutic counselor listed above and relate them to the pages of the New Testament, we will discover that the person we call Jesus Christ, as we meet him in the pages of the New Testament and in personal, existential "I–Thou" encounter today, has every one of them to an amazing degree—in fact to an infinite degree. It was exactly these qualities of Jesus' personhood which Mary Magdalene, Zacchaeus, the woman at the well, and others experienced in such a way that the encounter with him totally changed their lives. His infinite love embraces the sinner in a saving, freeing, joyous relationship.

Roberts, though operating independently of Truax and Carkhuff, confirms their findings and applies them to the existential situation of humanity. Roberts opens chapter three of his study with the question, "Why does psychotherapy work?" And he answers, "The simplest answer is that it provides a situation in which a person can be completely honest with himself and with a fellow human being."[21] The key is being in relationship with a person who has the quality of life and personality which enables the client to let down his/her defenses, see himself/herself as he/she is, see reality, and in this relationship become a whole person.

Training is certainly important to the professional psychotherapist, but is not the essential ingredient. We all know of cases where a marvelous transformation has taken place in an encounter with an adequate, loving person who has had no psychotherapeutic training.

Every one of us, from infancy forward, out of both pleasurable and painful experiences, build up a world of unreality which hardens as we grow older. Whether we describe this unreality in psychological or theological terms, there is the reality of "unreality" in every life. For some it becomes so critical that life breaks down and ceases to function. Whatever the source of help or "therapy" short of the divine "Wonderful Counselor," the cure or healing is always partial. In psychotherapy the counselor is always human, and is thus never completely adequate. Hence, recovery is never fully complete in every detail. The degree of completeness will be seen to be in direct proportion to the adequacy of the counselor.

In regard to salvation in the Christian sense, Jesus Christ is the "Wonderful Counselor," the perfect and completely adequate counselor. Therefore, he is the Savior, and the salvation he brings is complete for eternity. The only limitation here is whether the person coming to him truly surrenders. This is an existential, experiential testimony—not an argument. Roberts says of psychotherapy, "In a word, therapy offers a human relationship in which the false-front is no longer necessary."[22] This, which happens imperfectly in relationship with a human counselor, happens perfectly and completely in the relationship with the divine–human Counselor, Jesus Christ, the only limiting factor being the quality of surrender of the one coming. Here we have a definition of repentance, complete openness, trust, surrender, and faith. It is this saving faith that opens the person to full salvation, which is, through grace, the gift of God.

The most amazing and joyful discovery one can make is when he/she comes into a personal relationship with the supremely adequate person, Jesus Christ, and discovers complete release and genuine freedom. "If . . . the Son shall make you free, you shall be free indeed" (John 8:36 NAS). Such a person discovers that, with his/her total self—including the worst—laid out in the open, Jesus Christ accepts him/her and loves her/him. Thus one experiences the grace of God, the free gift of God's love. It is the most overwhelming experience a person can possibly have. It is not merely the acceptance of, or the appropriation of, that which one has read about, even in holy scripture, or that which one has been told. It is certainly not a response to a claim or an argument, but a response to a person, Jesus Christ.

The person responding to Jesus experiences the realization that his sin makes no difference in his being accepted by Jesus and fully restored to joyous wholeness. He experiences for the first time that he can be just what he really is—and not be rejected. He/she does not have to cover up or present a false-front in order to gain approval. As this truth dawns on him, he has "a wonderful feeling of release from life-long pressures."[23] This is conversion. This is dynamic salvation. It is what Saint Paul found and expresses so eloquently: "There is therefore now no condemnation to those who are in Christ Jesus. For the law of the spirit of life in Christ Jesus hath made me free" (Rom. 8:1–2). That there is a mystical element of interpersonal relationship in this person-to-person encounter is clear. It is an interpersonal relationship with God.

Such a trusting, saving interpersonal relationship with Jesus Christ, however, is not easy. It must be stressed that our defensive structures, built up over years of protecting our egos, and maintaining our self esteem as a front in spite of inner guilts, conflicts, and inferiority feelings, are almost impossible to penetrate. Indeed, every circumstance which is perceived by us as a threat or an attack only hardens and toughens the defenses. We are "imprisoned within the old strategies of defensiveness, anxiety and the need to feel superior."[24] The only way out is the way of suffering, as Scott Peck has so eloquently stated. Salvation involves, in the words of David Roberts, a painful "facing and grasping, in feeling as well as in thought, of the deeply hidden causes of inner dividedness."[25] And "this coming in sight of the underlying aspects of a problem can be so frightening or enraging to a person that he breaks off the analysis."[26] Roberts points out that "This facing can be carried on healingly (i.e., redemptively) only in a relationship of acceptance, (i.e., forgiveness)."[27] This is exactly what Jesus, the Wonderful Counselor, does. He accepts and forgives. The entering of such a redemptive and healing relationship with the Supreme Person is, in my judgment, the only valid meaning of salvation in the Christian context. Jesus not only sits beside us as advocate, brother, and counselor, but sits for us on the mercy seat as Savior. "We experience this divine forgiveness as that making right of our lives which occurs when we turn away from fighting ourselves, and others . . . and turn trustfully toward the divine power which surrounds us and can work through us."[28]

One of the real problems in all of this is that many persons sometimes have difficulty experiencing and knowing that Jesus Christ is actually present and that they are in an actual interpersonal relationship with him, since he is now no longer enfleshed in a physical body. Most Christians believe in the

Resurrection, but have not translated this belief into Jesus' personal presence today as a living person. What Person Christology aims at is making this presence quite real, for Christ is present as a person, risen, living, and in relationship—a healing, liberating relationship—with all who recognize his presence and who surrender to him and enter into the therapeutic relationship with him. We are speaking about a literal presence as a person, as any living person is present. We are not talking about a figurative or symbolic presence as so many people use the term when speaking of Christ's presence. This is the missionary and evangelistic task. This is the church at work, for the church is God's body of witnesses to this reality. How far we as the church, God's mission in the world, have strayed from this task is evident in many ways. But for our purpose here it is especially evident in the whole history of the arguments and the claims to have the "exclusive," the "highest," the "best," or the "final" revelation, etc. Such claims are a measure of sinful pride, not genuine witness.

This interpersonal relationship with Jesus Christ as a living person is saving because it is healing and liberating. It brings wholeness, fullness of life, hence joy. What the theologian calls repentance, confession of sin, is a vital part of the process. Confession and repentance not only bring inner release and inner healing, but also restore a right relationship with God and fellow human beings. There is reconciliation with God through Christ in the same way that there can be reconciliation between estranged persons at a human level through spiritual, personal, or psychotherapeutic healing. Paul says, "For he is our peace, who has made us both one and has broken down the dividing wall of hostility" (Eph. 2:14). Salvation becomes dynamic. It is no longer simply a formal, static change of status before God as relates to whether one will go to heaven or to hell. It is no longer a matter of changing one's name from one list to another in God's book. The person is certainly saved for eternity, saved to a quality of life that is eternal, and since we believe in personal, conscious existence after death, the salvation includes heaven. But heaven is only a part of it, however important it may be. The basic salvation is the "new creation" that the person experiences both for this world and the next. Salvation in a dynamic sense produces what Saint Paul calls "the new creation." We are "born again." In the words of Roberts, "It cures guilt, not by putting forward ideas which assure men willy-nilly that they are 'all right,' but by releasing power which removes the causes of guilt."[29] Release from sin and the power of sin (guilt) over us comes through faith in and relationship with Jesus Christ.

THE INHERENT SOCIAL NATURE OF SALVATION

With this focus on personal salvation, however, we must be careful to stress that dynamic salvation is neither narrowly personalistic nor narrowly pietistic. It is clearly communal and social. The fact that salvation comes only in relationship with another person (Jesus Christ) clearly indicates its communal and social character. It includes, likewise, a vigorous commitment to social justice. It is both mystical and personal, bringing wholeness, integration, meaning, personal fulfillment, joy, inner peace. Yet, it is also social, changing attitudes, freeing the person from prejudices, and instilling a deep sense of justice, forgiveness, and love in human relationships and social systems. One who finds a dynamic therapeutic "saving" relationship with Jesus Christ will find it of necessity in community. Dynamic changes within a person produce dynamic changes in his/her relationships with others. Indeed the two cannot be separated. Where, to the shame of Christianity, there have been those who have claimed (and there have been many) a genuine conversion experience in which social, racial, and other kinds of prejudices and un-Christian attitudes were left intact, the salvation experienced was clearly of the static type and not dynamic. Likewise, the attempt to bring about social and economic justice without changing peoples' hearts, which incidentally is characteristic of many of the "social gospel" efforts today, neglects the roots of evil. It may have temporary success, but, as the whole history of Christian missions and the social gospel movement eloquently illustrates, such efforts are ultimately doomed to failure. Social reforms brought about in this way are the result of a "cut-flower morality," imported by some person or mission with a zeal to cure the ills of society. They are clearly paternalistic and "imposed" from the outside, no matter how lofty the ideals of the "missionaries." If the emphases on justice are not rooted firmly in the native soil through conversion of the people to Christ, the cut-flower morality soon fades and dies. "Personal salvation" and "social salvation" can only be spoken of separately for purposes of verbal analysis. In reality they are one. Roberts says:

> Permanent cures occur only insofar as a man finds forms of affection, respect and trust in which he can participate. Such values are "self-sustaining" in the sense that once they are experienced, a

man wants them, affirms those things in himself which promote them, and voluntarily renounces those things in himself which would destroy them.[30]

Here is an apt description in psychological terms of what Paul calls the new creation: "If any man be in Christ, he is a new creature. Old things are passed away; behold, all things are become new" (2 Cor. 5:17 KJV). The new creation, contrary to what some idealistically expect, is not perfection. Rather it establishes a relationship with a fully adequate living person and through this person with all other persons. It establishes a model for all interpersonal relationships, and for the totality of society, the "Kingdom of God." It sets in motion forces which give a new understanding of self and a new center around which conflicts can be resolved. Roberts says:

> In general, most people who are caught in serious conflict blame themselves for things they cannot help, and fail to move toward procedures which are within their power. For example, they scold themselves for an outburst of rage, anxiety or eroticism which, at the existing level of self-understanding, was quite inevitable; but they feel sincerely that they cannot face what lies behind their problems.[31]

A static salvation leaves persons precisely in this dilemma. They may believe that their status before God has been changed (now they are "saved") but nothing in a dynamic way has been changed either in them personally or in their social relationships. Dynamic salvation, on the other hand, is a dynamic transformation that removes man-made evils at the source by changing the man. And in words strangely reminiscent of E. Stanley Jones's lifetime emphasis on the Christian way as the way God has created us to live, that Jesus is "the Way" in everything.[32] Roberts says:

> The principles whereby man reaches harmony within himself are at once rational and animal, spiritual and physical. The destiny of man cannot be conceived apart from his linkage with processes at every level in nature. In this sense God moves through His creation. As Friz Kunkel has put it: "Creation continues."[33]

We are suggesting that salvation in the full and complete sense of that term is the "making whole" of the entire person. Sin and guilt are removed; inner conflicts are resolved; inner peace and tranquillity are restored; creative powers of the personality are unified and released. Whether we are thinking in terms of life here and now or life in the hereafter, or whether we are thinking in religious terms, sociological terms, or psychotherapeutic terms, the answer seems to be the same. Salvation, wholeness, healing occurs in relationship, and is the result of a healing interpersonal encounter. The completeness of the healing depends on the quality of the interpersonal relationship; and the quality of the interpersonal relationship depends on the quality of the personhood of counselor plus the quality of complete surrender (repentance) on the part of the client or "sinner."

The kind of quality, the kind of empathy, the kind of identification, the kind of "nonpossessive warmth" which the Truax-Carkhuff study talks about for the ideal human counselor is what we read about on every page of the New Testament. Jesus is the perfect person, and therefore the perfect "therapist"—the Savior. Truax and Carkhuff speak of the therapist "assuming the internal frame of reference of the patient." This is precisely what Jesus has done. In the Incarnation he became one of us. He has assumed our internal frame of reference. As the God–man he reveals God, for he is God. But he also reveals perfect humanity by assuming our internal frame of reference. The "I am with you always," which closes the "Great Commission," is an expression of the transforming, nonpossessive warmth of Jesus.

Yet, this warmth, acceptance, agape love is never mushy or indulgent. It is firm and demanding. Jesus never condones sin or wrong or injustice in any form. The condition of forgiveness and wholeness is transparent openness and complete trust—in a word, repentance. Just as the effective psychotherapist radiates agape love for the client and is warm and accepting, yet communicates unconditionally that change is necessary, so Jesus as therapist, in the traditional phrase, "hates the sin, but loves the sinner." There is nothing soft and indulgent in the interpersonal encounter with Jesus Christ. There is infinite love and absolute acceptance in warmth and empathy, but there is also the clear demand: Change is necessary. There is no "cheap grace." Many "nominal" Christians have never understood this. Many have made a formal acceptance of Jesus as Lord and Savior, but have never encountered him as a living person to allow him to be for them the divine therapist who truly saves and makes them whole. As Roberts points out in regard to psychotherapy: "A high percentage of those who begin analysis can be described as sincerely wanting to have all the inconveniences of their neuroses removed without relinquishing the neuroses themselves (Horney)."[34] The clear demand of Jesus Christ, the "Wonderful Counselor" is that the "neurosis" must go, not just the unpleasant symptoms. We are not saved in our sin, but from our sin.

As I have already pointed out, religious pluralism is totally irrelevant to salvation understood in this way, for such salvation comes in relationship with a person, not a religion or an institution. It comes through a dynamic, life-transforming personal relationship with Jesus Christ and not, in the words of Bonhoeffer, through "cheap grace," whatever the religion dispensing it may be.

IS JESUS THE ONLY SAVIOR?

But the question remains, in the context of Christian evangelism and religious pluralism, is Jesus the only Savior? Or are there others? Though I have referred to the issue earlier, I need to be more specific. I do not wish to skirt the issue; neither do I wish to state more than I am qualified to state. As we have seen, many insist today, in the context of religious pluralism and historical relativism, that there are many saviors. Even some Christian theologians, as we have also seen, surrendering Christian uniqueness and accepting religious relativism, affirm this view that there are many saviors. However, we have noted likewise that these Christian theologians frequently are operating on the basis of a quite truncated simplistic concept of salvation. From the above discussion, it should be clear that Christian salvation, understood in the full biblical sense is quite different from "salvation" as many understand the term, which is primarily as simply a formal "ticket to heaven" that can be "bought" anywhere—i.e. cheap grace. Let me say four things in regard to this question of other "saviors."

First, as already indicated, it would certainly be improper for me to try to assert what God can and cannot do, or what God has or has not done. We cannot limit God, especially God as understood in the Christian faith.

Second, if the Trinitarian understanding of the nature of God is correct, as Christians believe it is, then Jesus Christ is God in his saving, redeeming action: "God was in Christ reconciling the world unto himself" (2 Cor. 5:19). If salvation is as I have described it, then if there were some other "savior," it would seem to be obvious that either (1) the salvation spoken about in relation to the this other "savior" would not be the same as the salvation offered by God in Christ, for the personhood of the "savior" would be different and the relationship (salvation) would be different; or (2) this other "savior" would be identical with Jesus Christ. If it should be that God has expressed himself in saving action in some other place or on some other planet or in some other world in our vast universe, in a nominally different way from the person, Jesus Christ, then such an expression would have to be identical with the expression found in Jesus Christ, for God is God and can be no other than Himself. In this sense the question, "Is Jesus Christ the only Savior?" is a rather meaningless question with an obvious answer.

Third, however we may view the logic or the meaningfulness of this question, one thing I do know is that Jesus is *my* Savior, and I share this glorious experience with millions around the world who make the same testimony. I have claimed that dynamic salvation is found in a meaningful interpersonal transforming relationship with the divine–human counselor, Jesus Christ, and not in such things as "grace-filled moments in various religions," "encounters with ultimacy," or in other such religious experiences. Salvation, at least for millions, has been found in a dynamic encounter with the living person, Jesus Christ. This I know. And it is this to which I testify. As for me, and as far as I can see, for the entire world, Jesus Christ is the only Savior in the sense that I have defined salvation.

Fourth, Acts 4:12, "And there is salvation in no one else, for there is no other name under heaven given among men by which we must be saved" is probably the verse most frequently cited as expressing narrow exclusivism and bigotry by those insisting that we abandon Christian uniqueness and adopt a thoroughly relativistic view. I would like to add here a brief word about this verse. How are we to understand Acts 4:12? Paul Knitter, Roman Catholic theologian, for example, in his book *No Other Name?* simply dismisses it as the narrow exclusivism of the early church and not a valid part of the gospel. He asserts that there are many "names." Of course every person must bring to this Bible verse, as to any other, his or her own understanding of scripture, and I am quite aware that many persons seem to view Acts 4:12 as an expression of exclusivism. However, I believe that if we look at the verse in the light of the total witness of scripture, this is not correct. Along with Acts 4:12 we need to note the many verses that emphasize the universal love of God such as John 3:16 and John 6:37, "Him who comes unto me I will not cast out." Certainly whatever Acts 4:12 means, it does not mean to imply that salvation is dependent on correct phonetics or linguistics. We dare not try to put God in a box, and

I do not think that in Acts 4:12 God puts himself in a box.

Let us consider three points: (1) God is love, and His concern is for all persons: "Him who comes unto me I will not cast out." (2) God, therefore, wills the salvation of all persons. "God so loved the world . . . that whosoever . . . " (John 3:16). (3) In Acts 4:12, God is not restricting salvation, but simply telling us the "how." This "how" involves a dynamic, life-transforming process, not a static, formal transaction such as acquiring a formal ticket to heaven. If salvation is seen in static terms as simply getting a ticket to heaven, which view we have rejected, then Acts 4:12 may pose a problem. But we have tried to show that this is not salvation in the Christian sense. If salvation is much deeper and more profound than this, as we have insisted, then the verse has a vital place and is not an exclusivistic affirmation in the narrow classical sense of exclusivism at all.

We need to note, first, that "name" was used quite differently in biblical times from the way it is used today. Today it is simply a "tag" or a "label" by which we are identified. Not so in biblical times. Names carried tremendous significance, and the name and the person were identical. William Barclay says, "Hebrew thought and language had a way of using the name which is strange to us. By that expression Jewish thought did not so much mean the name by which a person was called as his nature in so far as it was revealed and known."[35] Barclay continues, "To believe in the name of Jesus is to believe that God is like him; and it is only when we believe that that we can submit ourselves to God and become his children. . . . It is what Jesus is that opens to us the possibility of becoming the children of God."[36]

As is noted in Matthew, chapter one, and elsewhere, the very name "Jesus" means "salvation" and is thus synonymous with God's salvation. The entire Biblical witness makes clear that salvation is dependent on one thing, and one thing only—faith, faith that is total surrender and complete trust in a person, God—faith that is witnessed to and validated by sincere repentance. "No other name" in this sense is not restrictive, but inclusive. It is not a statement reflecting a narrow bigotry, but a statement reflecting the universal love of God in giving his son to open the Way for all. No artificial requirements such as belonging to a specific religion (there was no "Christianity" to join at the time Peter spoke these words), no subscribing to specific beliefs and doctrines, are required. It is another way of expressing what Paul expresses in Ephesians 2:8–9: "For by grace you have been saved through faith; and this is not your own doing, it is the gift of God—not because of works lest any man should boast."

"No other name" is therefore an exuberant exclamation made by Peter in a moment when he was so overwhelmed by what had just happened to the lame man through faith in the name (person) of Jesus that he could hardly believe what he had seen. Certainly Peter was not in an argumentative mood. No one was there trying to be saved in a different way or by another name or another religion. The verse simply says that there is no other way except simple faith, surrender, and acceptance of God's free grace. However, by specifying the name or the "person" Jesus, Peter makes clear that though the grace is free, it is not cheap. This is the point to "no other name," or better, "no other reality." The reality through which we are transformed and saved is a costly reality. It comes through "this Jesus" (Acts 1:11, 2:23, 32, 36) who paid the supreme price of death on the cross—and only through this costly grace. God had worked a miracle through simple faith, but no one should think it was cheap magic or that it was done lightly. It cost a price. Peter's exclamation is in no sense an exclusivistic claim, but a simple recognition of the power and quality of God's salvation that can heal even a crippled leg through the simple faith on the part of the person, but also through the costly grace on the part of God.

Salvation in the name of Jesus is total and complete for this world and for the next because it is dynamic, living, vital. It is not a matter of joining a religious movement or having a decree pronounced that you are "saved" because you have joined a particular religious group or "religion." Peter was not intending to place limitations on God's power of salvation, but rather to proclaim that in the name of Jesus—God's salvation—all are welcome through faith. The lame man had simply believed and trusted in Jesus—no religious pronouncements were involved, no belief in some doctrine or authoritative religion required. The Bible closes with the grand invitation: "The Spirit and the Bride say 'Come!' And let him who hears say, 'Come.' And let him who thirsts come [let him who] desires, [take] the water of life [without price]" (Rev. 22:17 NKJV). If you want this salvation, healing, wholeness, liberation, joy, come. It is found in an interpersonal relationship with God through Jesus Christ, the "Wonderful Counselor" and Savior.

If you ask whether Jesus Christ (God) can be encountered in saving power other than in the Judeo-Christian historical tradition, the answer is that certainly God is not limited. We believe that Jesus Christ as a risen, living person in the "new creation" resurrected noncorporeal body is universal—an expression of the universal Godhead—and is present throughout the universe. As Supreme Person (Father, Son, Holy Spirit) God may appear where he chooses and encounter whom he will in whatever form he chooses. The question as to how and where God is encountered is one that only God and those who might be so encountered by him can answer as far the possibility and actuality of such an encounter is concerned. But it is clear that if, as I have maintained, God is truly a person—the Supreme Person—and if the person, God, is identical with the person, Jesus Christ, as I have also maintained, then if it is a salvation in which God is involved, Jesus Christ is involved, wherever and in whatever form or whatever religious, ethnic, or cultural group or tradition it takes place. This is the heart of Person Christology. And it is also at the heart of Trinitarian theology. As to the ancillary question (though from my point of view a different question) as to whether those not having heard of or known or received Jesus Christ will go to heaven, I am content to leave that in the hands of God. I am not authorized to speak for God in this regard and do not presume to do so. I can certainly trust the God I find revealed in Jesus Christ to do what is both right and loving.

Let us now look in more detail at what constitutes the Christian World Mission in an age of religious pluralism. The question I need to be concerned about is: "Why have they not heard of and known Jesus? Have I failed to be a proper witness in the world?" This is the burning question I am faced with.

Chapter Five
OFFER THEM CHRIST

THE HOW
OF CHRISTIAN MISSION

THE LAST WORDS OF JESUS TO HIS DISCIPLES WERE: "YOU SHALL receive power when the Holy Spirit has come upon you; and you shall be my witnesses in Jerusalem and in all Judea and Samaria and to the end of the earth" (Acts 1:8). Our commission as Christians is to be witnesses in all the world to the divine–human person, Jesus Christ, who is risen from the dead and living today. Jesus says: "You shall be my witnesses!" We are not to be witnesses to the church, or to Christianity, but to Jesus Christ.

It is safe to assume that religious pluralism is here to stay for some time to come and that we will have a number of different religions continuing to exist in our world through the twenty-first century. So Christian mission for the twenty-first century will of necessity have to confront the issues of religious pluralism. Of prime importance in a world of religious pluralism is that we seek to build friendships and good relationships among adherents of all religious faiths in a growing world community. This acceptance of persons of all religious faiths, making for closer relationships and friendships among all peoples, does not in any way impede the Christian mission in our world. In fact, it promotes goodwill and increases opportunities. This is so because Christian mission is Christ-centered, not church-centered nor religion-centered. We are not involved in a competition with other religions. We simply go about our mission in a mature, friendly way to "offer them

Christ." We are enthusiastic witnesses and advocates of what we believe is true and enriching to human life, and we certainly expect others to be and do the same. Any idea of proselytizing on the part of anyone is entirely out. So we are basically and simply sharing good news. The democratic approach to Christian world mission has been made quite clear in what we have said above. We are simply to "offer them Christ."

We are not commissioned to promote "Christianity" or to make claims about "Christian uniqueness" or about Jesus Christ. We are not to argue that Jesus Christ is "final," "unique," "absolute," "superior," etc., though we may believe that any or all of these are true. We are not to promote the church or to solicit church members, though the church is certainly important. We are not to try to develop a theology which will solve the problems of the relationship of the Christian faith to other religions either through finding "complimentary values" and "convergent paths"[1] or through finding that "Christ" is somehow in their religions, making those religions "ways of salvation," as Raymundo Panikkar seeks to do.[2] We are not to "sell" Christianity or to make people into "Christians" in the nominal sense of the word. We are certainly not simply to make them members of the church, though if this comes about of their own free choice and their own free will, we rejoice. Rather, the goal is to introduce them to Jesus Christ, challenge them to receive Jesus Christ as a personal Savior, to encounter him as a living person, and to allow him to do his work with them and in them, transforming them into "new creations." Thus they become "Christians" in reality as well as in name. Our concern is that they become Christian, that is, followers of Christ, not that they become in a nominal sense "Christians."

Lesslie Newbigin has put it well when he says, "I meet [the non-Christian] simply as a witness, as one who has been laid hold of by another and placed in a position where I can only point to Jesus as the one who can make sense of the whole human situation which my partner and I share as fellow human beings."[3] The task is making Jesus Christ known to a person and the person known to Jesus Christ, who is already present. The one witnessing actually is no more present at the place of witness than is Jesus Christ himself. The only difference is that in every encounter the one witnessing is corporeally present, while Jesus Christ is noncorporeally present—and we must stress that he is present ontologically as a person, not present as a vague *logos* or "spirit" or "influence." If this sounds quite mystical, it is. But it is also in harmony with the possibilities inherent in modern physics as we saw in chapter three. We do and will always have a certain difficulty in transcending the natural limitations of thought inherent in our being, in the present life, bound by space and time. How can we encounter one who is present but not in a physical body? This is a mystery. But it is the cornerstone of Person Christology and Encounter Soteriology. We believe that it is a reality that is open to everyone who will come to know Jesus Christ and surrender to him.

The missionary or evangelistic task, then, is this: The corporeally present person, the witness—missionary, evangelist, layman, or clergy and the non-corporeally present person, Jesus Christ, in constant communication with each other, are involved together in witnessing, by word and sacrament, by deed and service, by empowerment and advocacy and in whatever other ways Jesus Christ directs. In short, we witness by "offering them Christ." We also need to be aware that witness is more than simple word of mouth. The human witness will: (1) introduce persons to Jesus Christ and seek to make those to whom he or she is witnessing aware of Christ's presence in person, primarily through the way she/he lives and acts as well as by word of mouth. This is where the Bible is crucial, not as a textbook for arguments, or proof texts for doctrines or sermons but as the source of knowledge about Jesus; (2) challenge persons to communicate with and become involved with Jesus Christ as a living person. This is the heart of prayer, meditation, and Bible study; (3) challenge persons, once they have come to know him, to surrender their lives totally to Jesus Christ in repentance and faith, to truly encounter him, and to receive him as personal Savior. Such surrender brings a deep interpersonal relationship with Jesus resulting in release from bondage to sin and release to the joy of Christian living; (4) challenge persons to live in the awareness of Christ's presence daily by allowing Christ to live in and through the witness, and thus to become involved in loving all persons of whatever class, race, gender, or religious persuasion. Such living and loving involves Christian community and relating to all persons of whatever status, race, religious, ethnic, or national background. This means that the witness will be engaged in service to others and in the struggle for peace, justice, liberation, and empowerment for all people, keeping in mind that we serve not a movement, nor a theology, nor an ideology, nor an institution, but a person, Jesus Christ, who loves us, loves all persons in the world ("God so loved the world that He gave his only Son" John 3:16) and is with us in person daily sharing our struggles: "Lo, I am with you always" (Matt. 28:20); (5) but, most of all, the human witness must be Christ's presence in the sense of the loving interpersonal relationships she or he establishes. The non-Christian must see, feel, and experience Christ's presence in the witness. This of course means that the witness must live a life of prayer and constant intimate relationship with Jesus Christ.

Mission in this sense does not involve a comparison of religions or of "saviors." It does not necessarily involve belonging to an institution, even the church, though belonging to the Christian community in some form is vital, and ordinarily the Christian will be a part of some church or Christian community. If the person is isolated in a community other than Christian, he/she through witness can in time form his/her own community, for community is crucial to the Christian life, and I am in no way minimizing it. In fact, this approach could definitely assist in dealing with one of the most persistent problems of Christian missions, namely that of importing "foreign" forms of the "American" or "western" church that do not fit into the culture. One of the most persistent and valid criticisms of the Christian mission today is that often it spreads "western culture" more than the Christian Faith. Indigenization, contextualization, and inculturalization (without syncretism) is one of the most important tasks of missions today.

This approach allows Jesus to encounter and witness on his own through his holy word and through the lives and witness of his disciples. We have faith that he, if introduced in a vital dynamic way, can accomplish the task himself through all of those who are his disciples, his "witnesses." He has honored us by making us essential to his work. We do not need to make claims about uniqueness and finality, which may show not faith, but lack of it (whistling in the dark). We really in fact and in deed need to trust in him to accomplish his work through his word and sacrament, through our proclamation, service, and advocacy, and through the faithful witness of all those who are committed to him.

Since we are writing on Christian mission in the context of Person Christology and Encounter Soteriology, we need to spell out the implications of this view for Christian evangelism and the relationships of Christians with other religions. It is our belief that the Person Christology and the Encounter Soteriology proposed here eliminate the untenable and un-Christian superiority position at the heart of both the exclusivistic and the inclusivistic positions which make the institution, not Jesus, the center. It does this because it does not make claims but simply witnesses and says, "taste and see." When the focus is on Christianity (a combination of God's revelation and our response), we are involved with "our" institution, our religion, and pride easily slips in. Jesus stands on his own. We had nothing to do with his coming. We can take no pride here. We can only share in grateful humility. Person Christology and Encounter Soteriology also make it possible for Christians to express what they have experienced in Jesus, that is, that he is both Savior and Lord—and the *only* Savior and Lord—without arrogance or a superiority complex. Person Christology and Encounter Soteriology do two things.

First, they place Christianity on the level with all other religions as one among many. They make clear that there is no claim that Christianity is superior to other religions or that Christians are superior to others. This may in fact be true in certain cases, but who is to judge? And it is certainly not our claim. The fact is that, depending on the kind of criteria used, Christianity, like other religions is superior in some respects and inferior in others. And certainly Christians are ordinary human beings like all others, sinners saved by grace. We agree with Hendrik Kraemer, misunderstood as the archexclusivist, when he says:

> Christianity is therefore not absolute. It is not even in all respects the "best" religion, if by that we mean the religion which has found, comparatively speaking, the "best" and noblest way of expressing religious truth and experience. During those parts of my life spent amidst other religions it has struck me many times that certain religious attitudes and emotions are more finely expressed in those religions than in Christianity. That is plain for any fair-minded man to see; and one has a duty to say so and to give honour where honour is due.[4]

Kraemer then proceeds to give illustrations such as the Muslim emphasis on the sovereignty and majesty of God: "Allahu Akbar" (God alone is great). He stresses the deep yearning for truth in Indian religions, as witnessed by the pilgrimage of Mahatma Gandhi. The obvious but often unrecognized problem in declaring Christianity or any other religion "superior" is the question of criterion. Depending on the criterion or criteria used, any given system may be better than, equal to, or worse than any other system. To assume Christian values as the criterion for comparison, and then declare Christianity superior is not only arrogant, but also involves a serious flaw in logic—the fallacy of *petitio principii* or "begging the question." Yet, this is what many Christians have consistently done. Also to assume western philosophical "enlightenment" concepts and values as the criterion (which John Hick and others do) is both arrogant and unfair.

Person Christology removes all of this subterfuge and declares frankly that Christianity is not superior. It is simply one religion among many with both "good" and "bad" in it, depending on what aspects are looked at, and what criterion or criteria are used. Of course, if we wish, it is possible for representatives of different religions to agree on a broad set of criteria and on the basis of these criteria to compare religions. Frequently interfaith dialogue follows this pattern. In such a procedure some religions score higher on some issues, and others higher on other issues. When done in a friendly spirit of fellowship, of seeking better understanding, and of getting better acquainted and thus building friendships, such dialogue has its value. But the danger is that it can tend to foster an unholy pride, create hard feelings, and even resentments if not done with great sensitivity and tact. It can be counterproductive.

Second, Person Christology and Encounter Soteriology focus on the living person, Jesus Christ. They simply present him as we find him in the New Testament and in our personal experience with him, and then allow him to stand on his own, saying basically to others, "taste and see." This is extremely important. Harvey Cox of Harvard University, one of the most astute liberal theologians of our day, discovered, as we will note in the next chapter, the importance of Jesus in interfaith dialogue. If in interpersonal, existential encounter you experience him as the divine power, as God, then you will know. If not, then not. It is not for me to make claims. My task is to introduce you to him and make him fully known to you. I recognize that a fine line is being drawn here, the line between a testimony and a claim. But this line must be drawn, and Christians must observe it ever so carefully.

What I witness to as a personal experience of encounter with the divine–human person, Jesus Christ, of course involves what I know about him, what I believe about him, and what my existential experience with him has been, just as it would with any person I might meet. And this experience of the divine–human person Jesus Christ can be so overpowering that my speaking about it can easily slip over into becoming a claim as over against other religions, and can be stated as such. This kind of subtle self-deception must be scrupulously avoided. The Christian may state what he or she believes, and what he or she has experienced, but should do it in such a way that it is a witness, a testimony, not a competitive or argumentative claim. This is why dialogue should be composed of testimony, never argument or comparison of doctrines and beliefs in a confrontational way.

We should make clear that the approach I am proposing in no sense means that I personally surrender my firm belief that Jesus Christ, the divine–human person, is God's self-disclosure of himself and of his will for all humankind. This is my truth-claim, my absolute, as explained in chapter one. It is one thing to hold a firm belief which one has put to all the rational and experiential tests he/she knows, and has found it confirmed by all that is going on in his/her own personal experience and in the world at large. It is another thing to make arrogant, boastful, or argumentative claims about the superiority of that belief, or the object of that belief. The only proper challenge is: taste and see. The approach of Person Christology by focusing on the living divine–human person, Jesus Christ, sets the question, "What is really true?" in the right context—the context of the living, pulsating world of today, dominated as it is by secularism. It places over against this secular pluralistic world the total Christian vision of life as experienced in the person, Jesus Christ and the Kingdom of God. It then says simply: taste and see. "What is really true" will be found in rubbing elbows with reality. This is what I have labeled above as the "scientific approach" as it was expounded and followed by the late Dr. E. Stanley Jones, a lifetime missionary to India and the world.

One who encounters Jesus Christ confronts a person—not a doctrine or a belief or an institution. She/he is faced not by a claim that can be debated, but by a person who calls for a personal response and decision. If the one who is confronted wishes not to behold, or not to respond, then all the arguments in the world, even if one wished to make them, are meaningless. I will be glad to witness, to tell you of the marvelous things I find in Jesus' friendship, his forgiveness, and his love. I will be glad to tell you how he has changed my life. But I will not compare or argue. If there is comparison in this sense of argument, you will have to make it. Of course I am not blind. I see comparisons, and in religious dialogue, the exploration of the similarities and differences in the doctrines and beliefs of the various traditions can be an interesting and sometimes helpful exercise. But I will not indulge in comparison in an argumentative way.

The main value in dialogue that focuses on the beliefs and practices of the various religions, is simply getting to know persons of other faiths, becoming informed and knowledgeable concerning their faiths, making friends, sharing fellowship, and creating lasting friendships. My only desire is to witness to what I have experienced. Furthermore, I welcome your witness to whomever or whatever you wish to witness, to what your religious faith means to you and to what your religious faith has done for you. I would like to hear what you believe to be true about life, the revelation you have received concerning the nature of reality, and what difference it has made in your life.

This is the essence of the "Round Table Conference," as proposed by Dr. E. Stanley Jones in his book *Christ At the Round Table.* I will sit as long as you wish, and hear your witness with as open a mind as I possibly can. I say "possibly can" because I will not delude myself that I can "jump out of my skin," shuck off who I am, and take a so-called "objective," neutral, uncommitted, philosophical stance as some philosophers and scientists claim to do. I will be not only open to you, but also open to who I am, recognizing as best I can my biases and faith commitments. This is the only way to be truly open, and being thus open I will be genuinely enriched by your witness. As John Donne said, I am a part of all that I have met. I cherish your witness in the same way that I cherish the opportunity to give my witness.

In the final analysis it must be that each of us as both rational and emotional beings must decide what resonates with our deepest understanding and our deepest feelings—that is, what "makes sense" to us, as we are guided by Holy Scripture, the Holy Spirit, and the minds God has given us. Here for Christians, the John Wesley "Quadrilateral"—scripture, tradition, reason, and experience—can be a helpful guide. Others will have their guides. In this way each of us comes to a conviction as to "what is true," based on the revelation we have received, which for me is the revelation in Jesus Christ, confirmed by the totality of our experience of reality.

I have no hesitancy in stating what I believe to be true and in standing behind it. I in no way surrender to relativity. In fact, I do exactly the opposite. Based on biblical revelation, I believe that there are certain values and principles that are eternally right because they are in harmony with the way the universe is made and thus are expressive of ultimate reality, as revealed in Jesus Christ and confirmed by the experience of reality.

In this sense "what is really the case" in reality is of vital importance for the totality of life, including "salvation." A relativistic view which says that what is true does not really matter, that one way or path is as good as another, may be just as tragic as is expressed in the lines,

> She thought she was drinking water,
> But she will drink no more.
> For what she thought was H_2O
> was H_2SO_4.

What is really true does matter. This reality is experienced in my own life as I submit to and follow Jesus Christ as Savior and Lord. The values and principles I find expressed and exemplified in the life of the risen living divine–human person, Jesus Christ, are the values and principles I hold. In other words, we cannot avoid the question of truth, i.e. what is really the case in reality. This is vital, and it is important that we understand the revelation in Jesus Christ, which I believe is reality.

In sum, I witness to the presence of a person—a living person who is here with me, though not in the old creation physical body. Rather, he is present in the new creation resurrected body. I have pointed out earlier that a human person is not the physical body one sees or encounters through any of the five senses, but is the invisible thinking, self-conscious, self-transcending, self-directing being one experiences through what we might call for lack of a better term, the sixth sense, i.e. the awareness of the presence of another person, be that person human or divine.[5] Martin Buber speaks of this person-to-person relationship as the "I–Thou" relationship. In Person Christology we focus on this invisible, but none the less real person, Jesus Christ, witnessing to his presence in our relationships with those of the Christian faith, of other faiths, or of no faith. And, again, in order to do this we must live with him both in the New Testament and in a constant interpersonal relationship today.

But again you may wish to charge that I have not escaped the implied superiority claim in that, as indicated above, Jesus Christ is viewed as the God–man and hence, by implication, is superior to all others. In reply to this charge, I say four things: First, I freely confess that my belief is that Jesus Christ is God and is thus superior to any human person. However, second, though it is my personal experience (I stress "my"), that he is the only "God–man" or divine–human person in this world, I have been careful not to say the only possible God–man, which would be to try to state what God can and cannot do. To make such a claim would certainly go beyond my knowledge and would be stating more than I can possibly be justified in stating. I know not how God may have chosen or may choose to reveal himself in other worlds or even in this world, or on other planets or in other times. I cannot put God in a box. I do not know all that God in his infinite wisdom has done or may do. But it is my experience that if God has revealed or may reveal himself in any other personal way, such revelation would be identical with Jesus Christ, for God is God and can be no other.

Third, I do know what God has done for me. I freely confess that in Jesus Christ, God has encountered me and continues to encounter me. This is a personal testimony to an interpersonal encounter—living person with living person. If this be considered mystical, it is. It is real. But, as stated above, it is also quite consistent with the findings of modern physics and the modern scientific age. Jesus Christ is the God–man, the Redeemer, the Savior I know. God has met me in Jesus, totally changed my life, and I witness to this fact with deep humility and gratitude, firm commitment, and unbounded enthusiasm not only as a past event, but as a present and continuing relationship. I make a faith statement, a testimony, not an argument. In him I have found what I believe is the real nature of God, that is, who God really is, as well as the nature of all ultimate reality, and I believe anyone who meets him will find the same. In John 14:9 Jesus says, "Whosoever has seen me has seen the Father."

In Jesus Christ I have seen God. I have found reality, the reality of the world around me, how it is made to work: "All things were created through him and for him . . . and in him all things hold together" (Col. 1:16–17). Also I have found expressed in his life the real nature of human existence as I believe God intended it in creation—the Image of God in human life. Jesus Christ is the Way—not just the way to heaven, but the way in everything. I have stated that Christians should not make argumentative truth-claims. But one claim—and only one—I do make, though in no sense an argumentative claim: Jesus Christ is Lord of my life. I further believe that if others encounter him—really encounter him—he will become Lord of their lives too. But this is for them to discover in surrender to him, not in claims or arguments from me.

Fourth, Jesus does not in any sense belong to Christians. The Christian faith is not "our faith." Jesus is not ours. Rather we are his. Therefore pride is totally out of place. The only proper attitude is humility and gratitude. The Christian refuses to get into the comparison game. He simply and humbly cries: "Ecce Homo," ("Behold the Man." John 19:5)—whom he believes according to the Bible and according to his own personal experience is also God—and leaves comparison, if there is to be any, to others. All talk of "crowning" or "fulfilling" other religions, or the use of such terms as "finality," "normative," "authoritative," "authentic," "anonymous Christians," etc. is out of place. The terms such as "anonymous Christians" and "ordinary ways of salvation" (applied to other religions) come out of an institutional hang-up on the part of Christians. Pride, arrogance, implications, or claims of superiority for Christianity must be removed. We simply sit down with others to witness to a personal encounter we have had, to tell others about a person we know, and to gratefully receive whatever witness they may have for us. We simply "offer them Christ." We believe that this provides the basis for genuine openness and for genuine dialogue. It is the way that E. Stanley Jones followed in his "Roundtable Conferences."

It is true that there are problems in such openness. John Cobb expresses the dilemma when he points out that

> It is not enough to recognize that different communities hold different views and that all are to be equally tolerated. Christians cannot continue to be Christians without believing that for them Christ is truly supremely important. But this leads to an opposite danger.
>
> If Christ is supremely important for Christians and if Buddha is supremely important for Buddhists, and if Christ and Buddha are different, then it seems that Christians must close themselves to the full meaning of the Buddhist claim, and vice versa, and that the thrust toward openness, inclusiveness, and universality that is present in both Christ and Buddha must be thwarted for the sake of mutual toleration. But when Christ becomes a principle of closedness, exclusiveness, and limitation, he ceases to be what is most important for the Christian and the appropriate expression of the efficacy of Jesus. In short, what would then be called Christ is in fact the Antichrist.[6]

Certainly Cobb is pointing to a fundamental problem. No person can be committed to two whole and entire religious faiths at the same time. As made quite clear in this entire essay, I agree with Cobb's statement that, "Christians cannot continue to be Christians without believing that for them Christ is truly supremely important." However, I must take issue with Cobb's statement that, "If Christ is supremely important for Christians and if Buddha is supremely important for Buddhists, and if Christ and Buddha are different, then it seems that Christians must close themselves to the full meaning of the Buddhist claim, and vice versa." This simply is not the case. Once we make Jesus Christ, the divine–human person living today, supreme in our lives, everything else fits into its proper place. We believe that the "Person Christology" proposed in these pages effectively deals with the dilemma Cobb poses since it eliminates the focus on beliefs, doctrinal claims, institutions, and comparisons, and focuses on witness to and relationship with a person, Jesus Christ.

For the Christian, to use Cobb's words, "Christ is supremely important." Yet, in the context of the Person Christology presented here, we can also be entirely open to Buddha. What we find in Buddha we receive gratefully—for example, his emphasis on inner integrity, respect for life, and nonviolence. This is his legacy, and a great legacy it is. But Buddhists certainly do not claim that Guatama was raised from the dead and is living today. The supreme importance of Jesus grows out of the fact that he is our "starting point," our presupposition, our absolute on which we stand. He was born, lived, and died in Palestine, is risen from the grave, and lives today as the divine–human person who has encountered and transformed our lives. At least this is my personal experience, my "starting point." If this is not true, then our entire house collapses. But we believe it is true. And this belief is not based solely on authority, though it certainly has the authority of the Bible. The belief is based on both the Bible and on our own personal experience with Jesus, thoughtfully considered and examined in the context of daily living as set forth above—the scientific approach.

Person Christology focuses on this fact: Christ's encounter with each one of us. It focuses on him, his person. And a person is a person is a person—an indivisible unity of rational and emotional consciousness. The person we are talking about is the divine–human person, Jesus Christ. The meaning of his uniqueness is clear so long as we stay with a Person Christology. He is not the "Divine *Logos*" or the "Universal Christ" or the "Creative Transformation" or the "Light that enlightens every man" or the "Cosmic Christ," though all of these expressions may be apt figures of speech that apply to him and his place and influence in the world. Rather, he is Jesus of Nazareth, Jesus Christ in person—in unique, resurrected person, with the nature of the uniqueness being that he was God Incarnate when in the flesh and is God present today in the resurrected, new creation body as the divine–human person without a material body.

This is a thoroughly Trinitarian affirmation, and we stress again that we must not get hung up on the linguistics of so called logical "contradictions." Whether we speak of Father, Son, or Holy Spirit, signifying different aspects and different functions and manifestations of the one God, however we may wish to express this, the meaning is the same: Immanuel—God with us. We stress again that this is a faith witness, which, though we certainly believe it is true, is not argued or pushed on anyone. We simply testify that we have met him, know him, love him, have experienced his love, and know that he can stand on his own. Our missionary and evangelistic task is not to "take Christ" to non-Christians, but to introduce him to them as a noncorporeal person already present but unrecognized and unknown, make him fully known, and let him stand on his own through his holy word and sacraments, and through his personal presence. In short, the missionary task is to "offer them Christ," and there is no task more urgent in our broken world. To a concrete example of this kind of Christian mission for the twenty-first century we look to the next chapter.

Chapter Six
OFFER THEM CHRIST

A MODEL

IN CHAPTER FIVE WE DISCUSSED THE BASIC NATURE OF THE CHRISTIAN mission today. The success of the Christian mission in the twenty-first century requires that we make the gospel relevant to our day and age. As we sought to make clear in chapter five, our task is not to promote the church or Christianity. We must simply enable Jesus Christ through our proclamation and witness to meet and to confront our age in the open market of religious pluralism, in what we speak of today as the "public square." The centrality of Jesus Christ and the "open market" approach were crystal clear in the evangelistic message and method developed by the late Dr. E. Stanley Jones. He worked in the most religiously plural part of the world, the subcontinent of India. So we will model our approach after his. As we will show, he simply followed John Wesley's admonition, "Offer them Christ." Stanley Jones's message and method are selected because they are ideal in the face of the pluralistic and relativistic challenge confronting Christian missions today. This challenge will be increasingly relevant as we go further into the twenty-first century. Jones began in India, but for over fifty years proclaimed the gospel around the world. His entire message and method were hammered out in a religiously plural society and are particularly appropriate for the kind of pluralism we face around the world today. Actually there is nothing really new about pluralism and relativism. Christianity was born in the midst of a religiously plural world, and even a casual reading of the New Testament makes this abundantly clear. However, pluralism takes on a definitely new character in our day.

Before going in some depth into Jones's missionary approach, however, we need to give a brief introduction to the man and the missionary. Stanley Jones was born just outside Baltimore, Maryland, January 3, 1884. He was educated in Baltimore public schools and studied law at City College before being graduated from Asbury College, Wilmore, Kentucky, in 1906 with an A.B. degree. He was a brilliant student and on graduation was asked to serve on the faculty at Asbury College. He taught for one year. However, he was already feeling a strong call to missionary service and in 1907 went to India under the auspices of the Board of Missions of the Methodist Episcopal Church. As was characteristic of missionaries going to India at the time, he began his work among the members of the very low castes and the outcasts. He did not attack Hinduism, Buddhism, Islam, or any Indian religion. He presented the Gospel of Jesus Christ, disentangled from western systems and cultures and their non-Christian, and sometimes un-Christian, expressions. "The Way of Jesus should be—but often isn't—the way of Christianity," he said. "Western civilization is only partly Christianized."

After a few years of preaching in India, Jones, because of his intelligent and reasonable approach, began to attract wide attention among the high castes, the students, and the intelligentsia. He was invited to speak at ancient universities and before learned societies. Soon he was set aside by his church to interpret the Christian gospel especially to educated men and women. In 1919 the Board of Missions of the Methodist Episcopal Church offered him the wide-ranging role of "evangelist-at-large" to India and to wherever else he might feel led, which subsequently proved to be to the far corners of the earth. Jones conducted great mass meetings in leading cities of India. At one such meeting, their leader, an Indian and not a Christian, said, "We may not agree with what Dr. Jones is saying, but we can certainly all try to be like Jesus Christ," clear evidence that Jones was making Jesus Christ, not Christianity, central in his message. He was "offering them Christ." He inaugurated what he called "Round Table Conferences" at which Christian and non-Christian sat down as equals to study the basic beliefs that motivate persons. Thirty years before the United Nations came into being, he proposed a "Round Table of Nations."

In 1925, while home on furlough, he wrote a report on his eighteen years of service—what he had taught and what he had learned in India. It was published in a book titled *The Christ of the Indian Road,* and became a best-seller. It sold over a million copies and has influenced the entire course of missionary thinking. Other books followed and certain books or single chapters became required reading in various theological seminaries or in degree courses at government colleges in parts of the world. They have been read around jungle fires, studied by armies and governments, quoted in parliaments, and banned and burned by Communists. In all, he wrote twenty-eight books, an average of one every two years for almost sixty years.

In 1928 Jones was elected a bishop by the General Conference of the Methodist Episcopal Church. However, he felt God had called him to the work of an evangelist and resigned on the eve of his consecration in order to continue his work as a missionary and evangelist. His work became interdenominational and worldwide. He held before persons the reconciliation of humanity to God and of humanity to one another through Jesus on the cross. He made Jesus Christ visible as the Universal God–man who had come for all people. This opening up of nations receiving Christ within their own framework marked a new approach in missions. It came to be known as "indigenization." He helped to reestablish the Indian "Ashram"[1] (or forest retreat) as a means of drawing men and women together for days at a time to study in-depth their own spiritual natures and quest, and what the different faiths offered individuals. Some came to refute the Christian gospel or to extol their own faith. Others found themselves accepting Christ's way of life. These confrontations of person with person and religion with religion greatly influenced the thought life of India's leaders and the views and activities of its ancient faiths.

Then in 1930, along with a British missionary and an Indian pastor, and using the sound Christian missionary principle of indigenization, Dr. Jones reconstituted the "Ashram" with Christian disciplines. This institution became known as the "Christian Ashram." Of course the Hindu Ashram is still to be found as an institution in the Indian religions. It is just that E. Stanley Jones created a Christian version of the Ashram. Stranded in the United States during World War II because the only overseas travel allowed was for the military, he transplanted the Christian Ashram to the United States and Canada where it has become a strong spiritual formation ministry.

Stanley Jones went to earth's trouble spots helping to promote international understanding. "Peace," he said, "is a by-product of conditions out of which peace naturally comes. . . . If reconciliation is God's chief business, it is ours . . . between man and God, between man and himself and between man and man." His efforts in Burma, Korea, and the Belgian

Congo and between China and Japan, and between Japan and the United States, to mention only a few, received wide attention. In the months prior to December 7, 1941, he was a constant confidant of Franklin D. Roosevelt and of Japanese leaders trying to avert war. In Africa, he was called the "Reconciler." On his first visit to Japan after the war, he was met with banners saying, "Welcome to the Apostle of Peace." He also won the esteem of all India. Men in the old British colony and in the new Indian nation, which came into existence after World War II, counseled with him. He had been so strongly outspoken for Indian independence before the war that for a time the British government had banned him from India. To this day he is spoken of in India as "The American Gandhi," a term of highest respect. His influence had no small share in establishing religious freedom in the new Indian constitution.

In India, Jones was involved in many activities in the various churches. He subsidized schools for lay leaders and provided "church extension gifts" to build churches and schools in Indian villages and cities. He also supported students of the Mar Thoma Church preparing for the ministry, students at Leonard Theological Seminary, Indian students studying in America, and itinerant evangelists and Christian workers in rural areas. The Mar Thoma (Saint Thomas) Church has now spread around the world with over a million members. Recently the Mar Thoma Church in Baltimore named and dedicated a building as "The E. Stanley Jones Memorial Building." Jones had a strong influence in preventing the spread of Communism in India. One of his books is titled *Christ's Alternative To Communism*. He founded, developed, and supported Sat Tal, a full-time ecumenical Christian Ashram as a spiritual center for India, Europe, and America.

An ardent supporter of Christian unity, in 1947 Dr. Jones launched a crusade for a "Federal Union of Churches." He conducted mass meetings from coast to coast, speaking in almost five hundred cities, towns, and churches. He advocated a system through which denominations could unite as they were, each preserving its own distinctive emphasis and heritage, but accepting one another and working together in a kind of federal union patterned after the United States system of federal union.

In 1950, Dr. Jones provided funds for India's first Christian psychiatric center and clinic, the now noted Nur Manzil Psychiatric Center and Medical Unit at Lucknow. The staff today includes specialists from India, Asia, Africa, Europe, and America who have given up lucrative practices to serve in this Christian institution which serves thousands of patients.

In 1959, Stanley Jones was named "Missionary Extraordinary" by the Methodist missionary publication *World Outlook*. He has been spoken of as the greatest Christian missionary since Saint Paul. He traveled among the peoples of the earth, speaking to all kinds of audiences, civic and governmental as well as religious. A heavy correspondence, writing a book every other year, and constant personal counseling, completed a program that went on round-the-clock, round-the-year, and round-the-world—a miracle of physical achievement. The years did not weary him, for he was blessed with physical stamina, mental vigor, and God's grace to sustain him in the rugged schedule he imposed upon himself.

In December of 1971, at the age of eighty-eight, while leading the Oklahoma Christian Ashram, Jones suffered a stroke that seriously impaired him physically but not mentally and spiritually. He was severely impaired in his speech, but dictated into a tape recorder his last book, *The Divine Yes*, and in June of 1972 gave moving messages from his wheelchair at the First Christian Ashram World Congress in Jerusalem. He died January 25, 1973, in his beloved India. Indeed, E. Stanley Jones was truly a "Missionary Extraordinary" to the twentieth century. He points the way clearly into the twenty-first century.

One clear requirement of mission and evangelism in the twenty-first century is that it appeal to both head and heart. Years ago on the mission field there were mass movements on the part of some non-Christians to the Christian faith based primarily on emotion and mass psychology. When followed by adequate instruction and discipling, such massive "heart" religious movements have in many cases become solid. However, for the most part, such evangelism is a thing of the past. Evangelism for the twenty-first century must focus both on intellect and emotion. This is one reason for selecting Stanley Jones as the model for twenty-first century evangelism. He very clearly stressed both heart and head. When he went to the mission field, he was convinced that his message had to be both reasonable and appealing. His Alma Mater, Asbury College, had given him a thorough grounding in the Bible and the fundamental beliefs of the Christian faith. However, his basic theology was hammered out on the mission field in the praxes of missionary engagement.

India, the birthplace of both Hinduism and Buddhism, was invaded around A.D. 1000 by Islam. For several centuries Islam controlled much of the life of India, and the Islamic religion was thoroughly implanted. Hinduism alone, with its "330 Million Gods"[2] provides a profuse religious pluralism. Add to Hinduism the other religions—Buddhism, Islam, Jainism, Sikhism, and hundreds of smaller sects, both ancient and modern—and we have probably the most religiously plural society in the world. This was particularly true around 1907 when Jones went to India. It is our thesis that the study of Stanley Jones's evangelistic message and method hammered out in this thoroughly pluralistic setting may give some guidance as we face the religiously plural twenty-first century. We look, then, at his guiding principles.

First, Stanley Jones's evangelism focused not on Christianity or the Christian church, but on Jesus. Also the focus was not on beliefs about Jesus or the doctrines and beliefs—the theology—of the Christian church, but on the person, Jesus, himself. Obviously these two are difficult to separate, and we are not suggesting that they either can or should be completely separated. Such separation would certainly be impossible. But there is a difference, and the point of one's focus is important. From the earliest days, the Christian community stated beliefs about Jesus, and these beliefs about Jesus, set forth in the New Testament, are of crucial importance. Stanley Jones held firmly to the basic biblical and evangelical beliefs of the Christian faith all his life. He believed in the inspiration and authority of the Bible, the Incarnation, the virgin birth, and deity of Jesus, the Trinity, the atoning death of Jesus on the cross, the resurrection, Christ's second coming, the fallenness of humanity, salvation by the grace of God alone through faith in Jesus Christ, and the church as the body of those joined to, and under the Lordship of, Jesus Christ. These beliefs were the bedrock of all his preaching and teaching. Yet, they were not the center. The center was Jesus Himself, the "Word become Flesh," the person, Jesus Christ, risen from the dead and living today. Some modern scholarship under the influence of Rudolph Bultmann and others has tended to view the resurrection as simply the "Easter Faith" that arose in the consciousness of the early Christian disciples. This modern view tends to speak of Jesus' presence today in terms of human consciousness as a vague "spirit" or *Logos* that pervades the world as a kind of power of "Creative Transformation" (John Cobb). For Jones, Jesus' presence today was simple. Jesus is a living person (He is risen!) with whom we can have an intimate personal relationship.

Jones went to India thoroughly grounded in the Bible. His message remained Bible-centered throughout his entire career, but with a definite shift of emphasis as a result of his encounter with India's religious pluralism. In his first book, *The Christ of the Indian Road* written after he had been in India for approximately twenty years, Jones says that as he went about evangelizing in India, he soon found himself "trying to hold a very long line—a line that stretched from Genesis to Revelation."[3] In the biblically-oriented western culture of America, defending such a line is at least a possibility. In the nonbiblically-oriented, religiously-plural culture of India, Jones found increasingly that it was a hindrance to Christian evangelism. After much struggle, he decided to give up trying to hold the entire line and instead to focus exclusively on the center, namely on Jesus Christ as the "Word become flesh." This turned some "fundamentalists" off. He was branded by many as a "liberal" or "modernist" and rejected. Jones held firmly to the authority of the Bible, but he rejected fundamentalist "literalism" and "verbal inerrancy." To use a modern expression, Jones interpreted the entire Bible Christologically. This means that Jesus Christ is seen as the center of the entire Bible. The Old Testament points to him and is interpreted in the light of his coming.

Second, Stanley Jones's evangelism focused not only on Jesus himself, but also more on what Jesus Himself preached than on what was preached about Jesus. In the context of a religiously-plural culture, Jones discovered what many Christian evangelists have overlooked: Jesus is not only the content, but also the model for preaching and evangelism. It is not that what was preached about Jesus is any less important. In fact, it is crucial. The early Christian community proclaimed the gospel—the "Good News" about Jesus recorded in the New Testament. This gospel about Jesus, who he was and is, is central to the Christian faith and proclamation. However, in preaching about Jesus, as important as this may be, one may fail to emphasize what Jesus himself preached, namely the Kingdom or rule of God and Himself as the embodiment, the incarnation of this Kingdom. Mark 1:14 says: "Now after John was arrested, Jesus came into Galilee preaching the gospel of God and saying, 'The time is fulfilled and the Kingdom of God is at hand . . .'"—at hand in Jesus himself. He was saying, "The Kingdom is here." He was himself the embodiment of God's rule. Living in harmony with Jesus Christ means living in harmony with God's rule; with the way we are made to live puts us in harmony with the universe and gives us an abundant life. Jesus said "I am come that they might have life and have it abundantly" (John 10:10).

God's rule is the great reality with which we human beings must come to terms. Jesus declared that this rule of God is absolute and all pervasive, controlling every aspect of both the physical universe and human existence.

If we wish to live well, to possess abundant, eternal life, we must live in harmony with the way God has made us to live. There are no exceptions. One of Jones's earliest books, *Is the Kingdom of God Realism?*, set forth and sought to demonstrate the thesis that all creation is made to function in Christ's way: "All things were created through Him and for Him. He is before all things and in Him all things hold together" (Col. 1:16-17). Rather than being an unrealistic idealism, as many suppose, Christ's way is the most realistic of the real. It is Reality with a capital "R"—Reality embodied in Jesus himself, the enfleshment of God who came to live among us. It is in this sense that Jesus is spoken of as the unique revelation of God, the absolute in a relativistic world. Whether any other person in history so embodies the revelation of God, that is, the way the universe is created to operate, is a question we will deal with later. But to our knowledge he definitely is such an embodiment, and, we believe, the only one.

Third, this means that Stanley Jones's evangelism focused not on religion, but on reality. A plurality of religions is thus basically irrelevant to his message. True, Jones was a Christian, but his message was not about Christianity or about a set of religious beliefs. It was about Jesus Christ as the embodiment of Reality. We say that Jones focused on Jesus Christ. Actually the ultimate focus was on Reality. Jones focused on Jesus Christ in no sense as "my religion" or "You must be saved through my religion"—a kind of "exclusivism" based on an arbitrary argument. Jones believed that Reality is enfleshed in Jesus Christ and that if you want to find reality, you will find it in him. The *Logos*—Ultimate Reality—actually became flesh and bones in Jesus Christ. Jones never put Christianity over against any other religion. He put Reality over against unreality and proclaimed that living in harmony with Reality meant abundant life, whereas living in accord with unreality meant destruction and death, both for the individual and for society. He certainly believed that we are saved through Jesus Christ. He dared to put this belief to the test of living, and found it to be true. Jones might be called one of the first "scientific" evangelists. He believed firmly in the scientific approach, that is, in putting the Way of Jesus Christ to the acid test of daily living.

The sciences of psychology and psychotherapy were just coming into their own during Jones's ministry. Jones's study of these disciplines together with his own experiences in counseling and his keen observation of the human scene convinced him that what is revealed in Jesus Christ is identical with what was being discovered about life, about reality by the psychologists. He found that what Jesus says about the way to live harmoniously, peacefully, joyfully, and abundantly is exactly what psychologists were discovering as the way to live harmoniously, peacefully, joyfully, and abundantly. Scientists were running head-on into the reality proclaimed by Jesus: It is only by losing one's life, by finding a focus outside of oneself, centering one's life in service to others, that the abundant life is to be found. Psychologists were beginning to preach what preachers had often failed to preach—that is, that a selfish, self-centered life is always an unhappy life. "He who finds his life will lose it, and he who loses his life for my sake will find it" (Matt.10:39). Hence Jones's over-arching emphasis on self-surrender. He has a book titled *Victory Through Surrender*. His many books, particularly his ten books of daily devotional readings, though some are as much as fifty years old, are as pertinent to life today as they were when written. This is because they simply "offer them Christ" as the Way to live—the way God has created us to live!

Following his explorations into psychology, Jones was emboldened to explore other social sciences—sociology, economics, political science, and the health sciences. It became clear to him that these sciences also confirm what God has revealed in Jesus. The Christian way is the right way in economics, in politics, and in all social, family, community, national, and international relationships. The health sciences and medical studies in general give abundant evidence that the Way of Jesus Christ set forth in the Sermon on the Mount and throughout the New Testament is the healthy way to live. Also studies show that the Way of Jesus Christ is the only way that will ultimately work in economics, politics, and other social relationships in general. We live in a world where human selfishness and sin have skewed everything in such a way that much of our social, economic, and political life is based on un-Christian principles. In such a skewed and twisted world the Christian way often seems idealistic and unrealistic.

But ultimately the Christian way is the only way that will work because it is the only way that is in harmony with reality. As stated above, reality is structured by Jesus Christ, and life will only work harmoniously if it works as it was structured to work, that is, in Christ's way. Just as an automobile will not run on water because it has been made to run on gasoline, so life will not run on hate because it is made to run on love. Life will not run on dishonesty because it is made to run on honesty. It will not run on selfishness because it is made to run on unselfishness. Jones's writings amass evidence, in the spirit of scientific inquiry, that the Way of Jesus Christ is the way—not just the way to heaven, but the way in everything, whether personal, family, social, economic, political, national, or international, and that this is evidence that Jesus is the unique revelation of God's will for the universe. This is the gospel, the "good news" of Christian evangelism.

There was nothing mushy or maudlin about Jones's evangelism. He did not use "tear-jerkers," exploit guilt complexes, play on emotions, or appeal to fear. He was always cogent and appealed to intellect as well as to emotion. He confronted the hearer with a reasoned and persuasive discourse on Reality and the way in which Jesus Christ is the incarnation of this Reality—the *Logos* (Reality) become flesh. Dr. William E. Berg, outstanding Lutheran minister from Minneapolis, Minnesota, describes Stanley Jones's approach as "evangelism without fanaticism; urgency without frenzy; proclamation without manipulation; promotion without pressure; enthusiasm without theological naivete; and personal regeneration with social concerns."[4]

This focus on reality rather than on religion is the key to the relationship of the Christian faith, and particularly Christian evangelism to other religions. In a sense it renders a plurality of religions irrelevant to the message of Christian evangelism. It means that Christian evangelism relates to other religions only as each relates to Reality and unreality. It is true that Christian evangelism, in Jones's view, asserts that Jesus is God incarnate, the embodiment of Reality, and for many non-Christians this will be seen as a dogmatic claim, bringing in a controversial element. But this claim is rescued from its seemingly "dogmatic" nature by the focus on scientific testing, as we have shown above. Jones held that the crucial test is the test of living. Does it square with the facts? Does it express reality? Is it in harmony with what we actually experience in daily life—personally, socially, politically, economically, nationally, internationally, and in every way? Is it the way to live? Is it the only way that will ultimately work? The answer to all these questions is "Yes." The focus is on Jesus Christ who is the Way—the way in everything, and not on belonging to an institution or accepting certain beliefs, though certainly faith in Christ is essential to following His way.

Fourth, Jones's evangelism therefore focused not on diatribe, but on dialogue. He never criticized other religions. He did not hesitate to discuss issues and to point to that which he felt was not in harmony with Reality, Jesus Christ, and thus not a correct reading of God's will and way. But it was always in the spirit of friendship and the facing of facts. He says, "I've been enriched through them [other religions]. Life can never be quite the same again." He respected and honored all persons and their religious commitments. His analyses were intellectually sharp, but he never cast aspersions. He never dodged the scandal of the Cross, but it was always presented in love, which is, of course, the major theme of the Cross.

Jones's favorite method of relating to persons of other religions was what he called the "Round Table Conference." Representatives of all religions were invited to sit down as equals around a table and to share their faiths. And it is interesting that many non-Christians not only participated in and supported such conferences, but joined in both sponsoring and leading them. There was no confrontation or tension. Everyone felt comfortable. The atmosphere was one of mutual respect together with friendly sharing and caring. Let Jones describe the "Round Table Conference."

> In our Round Table Conferences we gather about thirty people, the best representatives of the various faiths, and of no faith, and we say to them, "We have had the dogmatic, the controversial, the traditional approaches to religion. Shall we take an approach more akin to the method of science? In the scientific method there are three things: experimentation, verification, and sharing of verifications. We have been experimenting with this business of religion, using it as a working hypothesis of life. What have you verified in experience? What has become real to you? Will you share with us your verifications? I suggest that no one argue, no one try to make a case, nor talk abstractly, nor preach at the rest of us, but that you simply share with us what you have found in experience through your faith. If you have no faith, if you are an agnostic or an atheist, tell us how that is working. We will not sum up at the close. We will leave the facts to speak for themselves."[5]

Note Jones's emphasis on the scientific method. In an age when the warfare between science and religion[6] was still being waged in many circles, Jones boldly declared that we must use the scientific method in religion exactly as we do in other areas of life. He believed in, and championed revelation, but insisted that science was also a way to arrive at truth. The "truths" of revelation tried, tested, and shown to be true, and the "truths" of science insofar as they relate to the same area of life are the same, for truth is truth, however one arrives at it. One of his dictums was "Whether we come from revelation down or from the facts up, we arrive at the same place: Jesus Christ." He would agree with the astronomer who, in a moment of ecstasy while scanning the heavens through his telescope, exclaimed, "O God, I think thy thoughts after thee." He never feared putting the revelation in Jesus Christ to any test that can be devised, for he was absolutely sure that Jesus Christ expresses the reality of the universe. He was sure because across many years and in many diverse cultures and situations with individuals, groups, and nations he had used the scientific method, putting the Way of Christ into the test tube of daily living. He knew that the revelation in Jesus Christ would stand the test.

Much is being written today about dialogue with persons of other faiths as the wave of the future, and there is wide difference of opinion as to the value and place of dialogue in the Christian mission. Some Christians are presenting dialogue as a kind of substitute for proclamation and evangelism, the new way to relate to persons of other religions, which rules out evangelism. Others are seeing dialogue as simply a new strategy for a kind of hidden or covert evangelism, which amounts simply to proselytism. The first view ignores the Christian mandate of the "Great Commission." The second is dishonest and unworthy of the name "Christian." There are many proposals for dialogue today somewhere between these extremes. To discuss these different types of dialogue is beyond the scope of our purpose in this essay and would make the essay too long. But dialogue is certainly not new. It is precisely what Stanley Jones was doing in his "Round Table Conferences" with great effectiveness, and we will focus only on this type of dialogue since we believe that this is the fruitful way to dialogue.

In the Round Table Conference there was no pitting of one religion against another. There was only witness to what one's own religious faith has done and is doing in life. This is dialogue at its best—and evangelism at its best. In regard to the Christian's participation in the Round Table Conferences, the gospel is presented in the form of personal testimony. It is done in the context of a thoroughly democratic atmosphere that respects and honors each person's religious commitment. The Christian simply presents and talks about the meaning of his/her own personal I–Thou encounter with Jesus Christ as a living person today—not as a dead figure of the past whose teachings or example we may look back on and honor. All others are encouraged to share their own witness. There is no institutional focus, and indeed no focus on religion as such. There are no ulterior motives in terms of religious or institutional affiliation. All is focused on "What is Reality and have we found it?" "Is what I have found working in my life?" "Have I found joy and an abundant life in spite of problems?" "Have I found the way to live?" "What is the evidence of this?"

Of course, the Christian wishes for others the joy that she or he has found and she or he shares this joy with enthusiasm. It is precisely the Christian's contribution to the dialogue. For too long religious dialogue has been conceived of primarily in terms of talking about the religions, their beliefs and practices, etc., and how they relate to one another. The goal has been to get together and understand and appreciate each other better, which is certainly a worthy and necessary goal. But also we would insist that understanding and appreciation certainly cannot for the Christian be the be-all and end-all of dialogue. This focus, however, seems to remain the goal of most dialogue today. It is clearly the focus of Leonard Swidler mentioned above. Michael Barnes in his recent book *Christian Identity and Religious Pluralism*, with the sub-title *Religions In Conversation*,[7] presents dialogue in this way. In the section on "Dialogue In Practice" Barnes speaks of dialogue as a process of communicating and understanding ideas and concepts and that we must encourage the partners in dialogue "to look for common ideas and values."[8] The overall purpose of dialogue is "the pursuit of understanding."[9]

This need for friendship and understanding between persons of different religions is urgent, as we have made quite clear above, and dialogue for this purpose is extremely important. There is a need for persons of all ethnic and religious backgrounds to sit down together in mutual friendship to get to know, to respect, and to appreciate each other. This is precisely what we do in the city where I live, and in other cities all across the United States in interreligious "ministerial unions" or "ministerial associations," and they are quite effective.

Charles Foreman says of dialogue: "The purpose is mutual knowledge and growing friendship, the clearing away of prejudices and those ideas which are false or only partly true and in need of correction."[10] No one would disagree with this statement. But many, if not most Christians would not wish to leave it there. In certain contexts dialogue goes beyond this point. Stanley Jones insisted that we go beyond this "friendliness" stage of correcting errors and creating understanding, as important as it may be. Sitting at the Round Table together as equals in mutual fellowship and friendship, we can engage in dialogue that reaches to deeper levels of personal existence. The Christian's part in this dialogue is to make Jesus Christ known in a rational, intelligent, and compelling way as a real person living today, winsome, loving, not only demanding as the embodiment of God's rule, but redeeming as the loving forgiving power of God enabling the human race to meet God's demands.

This witness is made not only verbally, but also by winsome loving presence and service. Telling the story of Jesus and his love, making him known is crucial, but the witness must be more than verbal. It must also be vital. It must be a living witness. Others must see Christ in us. Likewise, it must be clear that argument over religions is absolutely ruled out. Of course participants representing other faiths have exactly the same privilege (and insofar as they feel it, the obligation) in regard to sharing their faiths. It is a thoroughly mutual existential dialogue. Jones had a profound belief that Jesus Christ as a living person would stand on his own and speak to persons if there was a genuine encounter. In fact, this is the ultimate faith in Jesus Christ. Jones makes the astounding statement after years of experience at the Round Table Conference:

> There was not a single situation that I can remember where, before the close of the Round Table Conference, Christ was not in moral and spiritual command of the situation. . . . wherever men are in fellowship with Christ in a personal way, this does happen, and it happens with almost mathematical precision.[11]

This is a very strong statement, and it is important to note in connection with it that the Round Table Conference strictly forbids preaching to the others or in any way seeking to "convert" others. It specifies that each participant can only share what his or her faith has done and is doing in his or her life. Immediately following the above statement, Jones says:

> There was no drawing of contrasts between the different disclosures of the adherents of the various faiths, no pointing out of superiorities by a clever summing up—we left the statements to speak for themselves, to be their own witness by their own worthwhileness.[12]

Fifth, and finally, this conviction led Jones to focus on personal existential encounter with the risen and living person, Jesus Christ, as the heart of evangelism. God's power to transform persons comes through the mystery of interpersonal encounter, not through any "thing," even the church, or the cross, or the altar, or the sacraments, or preaching, as important as all of these are. These "things" are instruments God uses. But salvation comes through the actual interpersonal dynamics of the encounter of two persons, Jesus Christ and the human person. This is the heart of Person Christology.

The goal of all of Stanley Jones's preaching was simply to introduce persons to Jesus Christ. "Believe on the Lord Jesus Christ, and thou shalt be saved" meant for him a personal encounter with Jesus Christ. "Believe" in this verse meant to him "faith," "trust." It was never a *fides quae*—accepting beliefs about Jesus—but a *fides qua*—a trust in and surrender to Jesus Christ as the "power of God unto salvation." The personal encounter with Jesus had transformed his own life, had given him a new power, and had brought unspeakable joy and fullness of life. He simply wanted everyone in the world to experience this same encounter with Jesus, the victorious joy that it brings to the individual, and the peace and happiness that it brings to the world. Remember again our paradigm of how an interpersonal encounter with Jesus can totally transform life. Jones insisted that every person, regardless of his or her accomplishments or character, needs Jesus Christ, and he carefully showed why. In an address given in Memphis, Tennessee, following the 1928 Jerusalem Conference of the International Missionary Council, he pointed to the exemplary character of Mahatma Gandhi, who was his personal friend, and asked the question: Does a great and good man like Mahatma Gandhi need Jesus Christ? The answer is, emphatically, "Yes," and the balance of the address seeks to show why. [13]

In preaching the Kingdom of God and Jesus Christ as the embodiment (incarnation) of this rule or Kingdom, Jones was clearly aware that God makes absolute demands: Live in harmony with God's rule or perish. But likewise he was aware that such a demand is impossible for fallen human beings out of their own human resources to meet. It is not that the human race has not tried. In fact, across the centuries persons of all races, religious, and ethnic backgrounds have struggled with great determination to meet God's demands. The noble teachings of the great sages of all cultures and religions, the lofty ideals of the great philosophers, the stirring challenges of the great moralists, the rigid self-denial of the great mystics and ascetics, and the unsurpassed devotion of the saints of all religions testify to the tenacious commitment of the human race to measure up to God's demands. Jones had a great respect for all the great religions and philosophies, the beauty of their precepts, and the nobility of many of their adherents.

But alas, the tragic experience of the human race has been that commitment and determined effort are not enough. The beauty of the ideals expressed in the world's great scriptures and philosophical writings only underscores the tragic wrecks of human history. The heroic nature of the human struggle to measure up only underscores the depth of human failure. With all the admonitions in the world's religions to integrity and rectitude, dishonesty and corruption run rampant. With all the exhortation to practice love and brother/sisterhood, strife and wars continue. With all the stirring essays on service to our fellow man, greed and self-seeking still control the human race. What more eloquent testimony could there be for the fact of what Christians call the "fall" of man or "original sin?" Can it be true after all that the human race really cannot out of its own resources measure up to the demands of God's rule?

The absolutely overwhelming evidence of history says a resounding "Yes." We cannot save ourselves. The great religions and philosophies point the way. But the testimony of humankind seems to be that only the trans-forming interpersonal encounter with Jesus actually enables us to find and follow the Way by giving us a new power. We must have a power from outside ourselves, and Jones presented the life-transforming encounter with the risen living person, Jesus Christ, as this power. How this power operates, how it happens that the person in interpersonal encounter with Jesus is transformed, is a mystery. But that it happens is a fact which cannot be denied. When such a transforming miracle takes place, "religion" as such is clearly secondary. Religion is important in the sense of a "community of faith" that nourishes, informs, and inspires through worship, ritual, educa-tion, involvement in service, and other forms that can lead persons to Jesus Christ. But "religion" as such, however it may be defined, is not the essen-tial thing. Rather, such a transforming interpersonal encounter is open to every person through simple faith and an interpersonal encounter with Jesus Christ risen from the grave and living today in person, regardless of the person's race, religious background, or ethnic and national origin.

This, again, is in no way to minimize religion with all of its heritage, ritual forms, and inspiring, sustaining worship and fellowship. But it is to make clear that the crucial, essential ingredient in a transforming experience is the interpersonal encounter with Jesus Christ. This is the heart of Jones's evangelism and also the heart and essential meaning of Acts 4:12, ("no other name") which we will discuss below. In a very real sense Jones was not a religionist, though he devoted his entire life to a religious vocation. In fact, he was what we might call an existentialist—though certainly not in the sense of modern philosophical existentialism. He was an existentialist in the sense that he focused on personal existence and on the interpersonal, I–Thou encounter with the living person, Jesus Christ, as the heart of the Christian faith and Christian evangelism.

Of course we need to be careful to underscore that evangelism for Jones in no way ends with this personal I–Thou encounter. This is only the beginning. Jones's dictum was "Evangelism that does not begin with the individual does not begin; evangelism that ends with the individual, ends." He stressed that conversion is both individual and social. There is no such thing as personal salvation apart from social salvation. A saving relationship with Jesus Christ must of necessity involve one in community with other Christians and in a saving relationship with society; thus, the crucial importance of the church as a fellowship of those surrendered to and committed to Jesus Christ. For Jones, the dichotomy between the so called "personal gospel" and the "social gospel" is a false dichotomy.

Jones's evangelism worked. He preached an average of three times a day, for over fifty years in nearly every country of the world, with time out only occasionally to write a book. No evangelist in modern times has been more active. Whatever the audience or congregation, he always preached Christ, never deviating in the slightest. Also, he never omitted or tried to gloss over in any way the scandal of the Cross. In fact, he always magnified it. "Self-surrender" and "You must be born again" were always at the center. Yet, he probably had more close friends among leading non-Christians than any other Christian in the twentieth century. This fact clearly refutes those who argue that we must soft-pedal emphasis on the uniqueness of Jesus if we are to relate to persons of other religious faiths. Jones said, "You cannot be more universal by being less Christian."[14]

In his last book he records:

> I once went to speak to the Rotary Club. I sat down alongside a Jewish Rabbi when I finished. I asked him, "Rabbi, was I too Christian for you today?" He said, "Oh no. The more Christian you are, the better you'll treat the Jews!" Whether it is Jews or nature or yourself, the Christian way is the natural way to live, and you find you are in your homeland the moment you become Christian.[15]

Note that he does not say, "a Christian," but "Christian"—that is, a follower of Jesus in your commitment and in the way you live. Harvard University theologian, Harvey Cox, one of the leading liberal theologians of our day and one of the chief architects of the secularization movement in theology, discovered to his amazement this fact which Stanley Jones had found earlier. He went on the dialogue trail and found that "Jesus is not merely a background figure. He is central to the Christian faith. Not only do the Christian dialoguers recognize this, but so do their Muslim, Buddhist, Shinto, Hindu and Jewish conversation partners."[16] Cox discovered that "any honest dialogue between Christians and others will sooner or later—and in my experience it is usually sooner—have to deal with the figure of Jesus."[17] He then continues, "My problem with dialogue tactics that play down the Jesus factor is that—surprisingly—it is just this factor that the non-Christian participants often seem most interested in and most eager to discuss. This is not something one is led to expect will happen in interfaith dialogue. But it does."[18]

Because of his Christlike character and openness, Jones became a friend of Mahatma Gandhi and spent considerable time at Gandhi's Ashram. He had many conversations with Gandhi and witnessed to him many times. Gandhi never professed faith in Christ, and this was one of the great disappointments in Jones's life. However, Jones was a true missionary in witnessing to Christ (not trying to "convert" Gandhi), and Jesus had a profound influence on Gandhi's life. Many have observed that Gandhi in his character and life was more like Jesus than the large majority of Christians. In this sense he was Christian, though not "a Christian" in the sense of affiliation with the Christian faith.

Jones also became a good friend of most of the major leaders of India following independence. The majority were Hindu or Muslim. I recall that once when Jones was visiting in the Philippines, where we were missionaries, a leading cabinet minister in the Indian national government had been invited to speak at the University of the Philippines. We attended, and when we went up after the address, the speaker saw us and blurted out, "Dr. Jones, what are you doing in the Philippines?" Jones was known, respected, and loved far beyond Christian circles in India. Gandhi was asked one day by a mutual acquaintance what he thought of Stanley Jones. His reply: "He is a very nice young man. But he is too sure of his religion." Jones was genuinely "Christian," devoted to Jesus Christ—not just an affiliate of the Christian faith.

Among Jones's twenty-eight books is an appreciative biography of Mahatma Gandhi, which is titled *Gandhi, Portrayal of a Friend*.[19] It is still in print. Martin Luther King Jr. told Stanley Jones's daughter, Eunice Jones Mathews, (wife of Bishop James K. Mathews of the United Methodist Church) that it was reading her father's biography of Gandhi which led him to adopt the strict nonviolent method in the civil rights struggle in the United States. Bishop and Mrs. Mathews have remained close to the Gandhi family across the years, forming bonds of friendship with the children and grandchildren that reach far beyond religious affiliation. The entire Gandhi family and indeed all of India have been profoundly influenced by the evangelism of Stanley Jones. This, in my judgment, is Christian evangelism at its very best and is a viable model for mission and evangelism in the twenty-first century.

Stanley Jones remained a fervent evangelist to the day of his death at age eighty-nine. He wrote his last book, *The Divine Yes*, from his deathbed by dictating into a tape recorder. Thousands came to a vital, life-transforming encounter with Jesus Christ through his ministry and thousands more have discovered under his preaching, through his books, and through the Christian Ashram ministry which he founded in 1930, more and more of the unsearchable riches of Jesus Christ. Jones was truly a "Christ intoxicated" man, a worthy model for evangelism in the twenty-first century. Following this model, Christian evangelism for the twenty-first century will enthusiastically present Jesus Christ to the world as God's revelation of himself, and as the model for the way God created humanity to live—that is, how things really are as verified in the burning crucible of daily living.

This evangelism will not only present Jesus as God's revelation of the way we are created to live, but also as the power of God through the cross and the interpersonal transforming encounter with the risen living person Jesus Christ to transform us and thus enable us to live as God intended. It will also create a support and growth fellowship (the "church" in some form) for those centered around Jesus Christ. We will become skilled in how to communicate as equals and to dialogue with persons of all cultures, all racial, ethnic, and religious backgrounds, as brothers and sisters. We will simply become the "friends of Jesus" making him known in a loving and winsome way to those who do not know him. We will carry out his commission: "You shall be my witnesses . . . " (Acts 1:8). Through the interpersonal transforming encounter and continuing fellowship with Jesus Christ, we and all those of whatever ethnic or religious or national background who come to him will be transformed, will receive power for living in the twenty-first century. We will find meaning, fulfillment, and joy both for this world and for the next. This is the Christian world mission for the twenty-first century. We will simply "offer them Christ" in as appealing, compelling, and loving way as possible. Can anyone doubt the urgency of this mission today?

ENDNOTES

Preface

1. John Hick, ed., The Myth of God Incarnate (Philadelphia: Westminster Press, 1977), also John Hick and Paul Knitter, eds., *The Myth of Christian Uniqueness* (Maryknoll, N.Y.: Orbis Press, 1987).

2. This centering of Christology in the resurrection is being increasingly confirmed. The recent book *The Real Jesus* by Luke Timothy Johnson, published in 1996 after I finished this manuscript, shows convincingly that the real Jesus is not found by picking to pieces the tidbits of information that can be gleaned from first and second century records, but in encountering the ressurected Jesus in the pages of the New Testament. This is indeed the "real Jesus," the Jesus we find clearly reflected in the canonical gospels.

3. Gerald O'Collins, *What Are They Saying about Jesus?* (New York: Paulist Press, 1917), 17.

Chapter One

1. David B. Barrett, "Annual Statistical Table on Global Mission: 1998," vol. 22, no. 1 of *International Bulletin* (1998), 26–27.

2. See such books as Paul F. Knitter, *No Other Name?* (Maryknoll, N.Y.: Orbis Books, 1985), also Hick and Knitter, *The Myth of Christian Uniqueness* (Maryknoll, N. Y.: Orbis Books, 1987), also Leonard Swidler, ed., *Toward a Universal Theology of Religion*, (Maryknoll, N.Y.: Orbis Books, 1987).

3. J. N. Farquhar, *The Crown of Hinduism* (London: Oxford University Press, 1913).

4. William Ernest Hocking, *Re-Thinking Missions, A Laymen's*

Inquiry After One Hundred Years (New York: Harper and Brothers, 1932).

5. Of course, since our focus as stated above, is not on religion with all of its phenomena, but on personal existence, this debate is actually irrelevant to Christian mission as we present it in these pages.

6. Hendrik Kraemer, *The Christian Message in a Non-Christian World*, 3rd ed. (Grand Rapids, Mich.: Kregel Publications, 1956).

7. This phrase, coined by Hick in 1973, appears repeatedly in his writings.

8. Lesslie Newbigin, "Religion for the Marketplace," Gavin D'Costa, ed., *Christian Uniqueness Reconsidered,* (Maryknoll, N.Y.: Orbis Books, 1990), 142.

9. Surin, "A 'Politics of Speech,'" Gavin D'Costa, ed., *Christian Uniqueness Reconsidered*, (Maryknoll, N.Y.: Orbis Books, 1990), 192–212.

10. Leonard Swidler, *After the Absolute* (Minneapolis: Fortress Press, 1990).

11. Newbigin, *Christian Uniqueness Reconsidered*, 143.

12. John Hick, Philosophy of Religion, 3rd ed. (Englewood Cliffs, N.J.: Prentice Hall, 1983), 101.

13. William Zuurdeeg, *An Analytical Philosophy of Religion* (New York: Abingdon Press, 1958), 28, 94.

14. For example, in response to the book, *The Myth of Christian Uniqueness* (Hick and Knitter), an article appeared in a religious journal titled "The Truth of Christian Uniqueness." I, too, believe Christ is unique, and believe it passionately, but it is still a belief, not a "truth." For the writer of the article in question, the word *truth* sounds so much stronger than the word *belief* in response to the loaded word *myth*. The ontological use of the word *truth* by phenomenologists and others must, in my judgment, be rejected because of the ambiguity involved. The only unambiguous—and, in my judgment—the only valid use of the word *truth*—is for that which is not false and which can be reasonably shown to be so.

Chapter Two

1. C. F. J. Williams, *What is Truth?* (Cambridge: Cambridge University Press, 1976), 1.

2. Thomas J. Altizer, William A. Beardsley, and J. Harvey Young, eds., *Truth, Myth and Symbol* (New Jersey: Prentice-Hall, 1962), 61.

3. Leslie Armour, *The Concept of Truth* (Assen. Van Gorcum-Comp., N.V., 1969), 1.

4. Emil Brunner, *Truth as Encounter* (Philadelphia: Westminster Press, 1943).

5. Elliott Deutsch, *On Truth: An Ontological Theory* (Honolulu: University Press of Hawaii, 1979).

6. Armour, 245.

7. Alan White, *Truth* (New York: Macmillan, 1970), 3.

8. Ibid., 3–4.

9. Deutsch, 66.

10. Wilfred Cantwell Smith, *Questions of Religious Truth* (New York: Charles Scribner's Sons, 1967).

11. Ibid., 77.

12. Ibid., 79.

13. Ibid., 67.

14. Ibid., 73.

15. Ibid., 69.

16. Ibid., 70.

17. Ibid., 71.

18. Ibid., 76.

19. Ibid., 68.

20. Ibid., 94.

21. However, it should be noted that the statement as of the time it was made remains false.

22. Smith, 75.

23. Ibid., 74.

24. Howard R. Burkle, "Jesus Christ and Religious Pluralism," *Journal of Ecumenical Studies*, 16:3 (1979), 461.

25. Smith, 83.

26. Lesslie Newbigin, *The Gospel in a Pluralistic Society* (Grand Rapids: William B. Eerdmans Publishing Company, 1989), 9.

27. Zuurdeeg, 28, 94.

28. We need to be aware, however, that these terms also involve a matter of testing or a matter of opinion: What do we mean by "authentic?" What is the test of authenticity and inauthenticity?

29. E. Stanley Jones, *Christ at the Round Table* (Nashville: Abingdon Press, 1928).

Chapter Three

1. J. A. T. Robinson, *Re-Dating the New Testament* (Philadelphia: The Westminster Press, 1976).

2. Rudolf Bultmann, *Theology of the New Testament*, Vol. 2 (New York: Charles Scribner's Sons, 1955), 59–69.

3. Raymond Panikkar, *The Unknown Christ of Hinduism* (London: Darton, Longman and Todd, 1968).

4. John Cobb, *Christ in a Pluralistic Age* (Philadelphia: The Westminster Press, 1975).

5. See such books as: John Hick and Paul F. Knitter, eds., *The Myth of Christian Uniqueness* (Maryknoll, N.Y.: Orbis Books, 1987), Paul F. Knitter, *No Other Name?* (Maryknoll, N.Y.: Orbis Books, 1985), and Leonard Swindle, ed., *Toward a Universal Theology of Religion* (MaryKnoll, N.Y.: Orbis Books, 1987).

6. John T. Pawlikowski, *Christ in the Light of the Christian-Jewish*

Dialogue (New York: Paulist Press, 1982), 119.

7. See endnote #5 above.

8. Wolfhart Pannenberg, *Theology as History* (London: McMillan, 1968), 104.

9. Ibid., 125.

10. Ibid., 142–43.

11. Lucien Richard, *What Are They Saying about Christ and World Religions?* (Maryknoll, N.Y.: Orbis Press, 1981), 16.

12. Ibid., 16.

13. Cobb, 139.

14. Alan Richardson, *Creeds in the Making* (London: S.C.M. Press, 1935), 75.

15. Cobb, 139.

16. Ibid.

17. John Hick, *Philosophy of Religion*, Third ed. (Englewood Cliff, N.J.: Prentice Hall, 1983), 11.

18. Richardson, 65.

19. Ibid.

20. The three examples of unusual talent given here come from "Sixty Minutes" 21:34, transcript (New York: CBS News, 1989), 8–12.

21. Immanuel Kant rather clearly demonstrated that we cannot know "the thing in itself" apart from our sensations of it.

22. Thomas V. Morris, *The Logic of God Incarnate* (Ithaca, N.Y.: Cornell University Press, 1986). Also one might look at the more recent, rather practical discussion of the issues in Millard J. Erickson, *The Word Became Flesh* (Grand Rapids: Baker Book House, 1991).

23. Morris, 105.

24. Karl Rahner and Wilhelm Thusing, *A New Christology* (New York: The Seabury Press, 1980), 14.

25. Rahner and Thusing, 26.

26. Bernard Ramm, *An Evangelical Christology* (New York: Thomas Nelson Publishers, 1985), 100.

27. Cobb, 20.

28. Gerald O'Collins, *What Are They Saying about Jesus?* (New York: Paulist Press, 1977), 17.

29. Also there is a recent rather practical discussion of the philosophical issues involved in the Incarnation by Millard J. Erickson, *The Word Became Flesh* (Grand Rapids, Mich.: Baker Book House, 1991).

30. Gilbert Ryle, *The Concept of Mind* (London: Hutchinson and Co., 1949).

31. From an article by David Gelman and others, "Is the Mind an Illusion?" *Newsweek*, 20 April 1992, 71–72.

32. Daniel Dennett, a thorough physicalist, states that there are six familiar themes, each of which

identifies "a necessary condition of personhood." 1. The first and most obvious theme is that persons are rational beings. 2. Persons "are beings to which states of consciousness are attributed." 3. There is "an attitude toward" or "a stance adopted with respect to a person." 4. To be a person, the being "must be capable of reciprocating in some way." 5. To be a person, the being "must be capable of verbal communication." 6. "Persons are distinguishable from other entities by being conscious in some special way." These are found in *Brainstorms* (Cambridge, Mass: The MIT Press, 1981), 269–71.

33. Borden Parker Bowne, *Personalism* (Norwood, Mass: The Plimpton Press, 1908), 265.

34. Richard F. Kitchener, ed., *The Worldviews of Contemporary Physics— Does It Need a New Metaphysics?* (Albany: State University of New York Press, 1988).

35. Bowne, 279.

36. In no way do I intend to indicate that being "personal," at least at the human level, can be separated from either the psychological or the social, but make this distinction only for sake of analysis.

37. Edgar S. Brightman, ed., *Personalism in Theology* (Boston: Boston University Press, 1943), 44.

38. Ibid., 45.

39. Ibid., 44.

40. Edgar S. Brightman, *Person and Reality, An Introduction to Metaphysics* (New York: The Ronald Press Co., 1958), 199.

41. Ibid., 41.

42. This is what Hick, Richardson, and others do when they object to speaking of God as a Person, but then speak of him as "personal." See pages 53–54 above.

43. Alfred North Whitehead and others, wrestling with this issue of the nature of ultimate reality, opt for the concept of "process" and develop what they call a "process" ontology. My problem with Whitehead's process philosophy is, How can "process" be ultimate? And if so, what would this mean? How can there be process without something in process? The term "process" involves of necessity both time and something in process. Also it involves some being (a person or persons) aware of it being "a process." Process itself cannot be "aware" of itself.

44. Bowne, 266.

45. Ibid.

46. Ibid., 269.

47. Ibid., 268.

48. Quoted by J. A. Wheeler and C. M. Patton in "Is Physics Legislated by Cosmogony?" in *The Encyclopedia of Ignorance*, Ronald

Duncan and Miranda Weston-Smith, eds., (New York: Pergamon Press, 1977), 20.

49. Bowne, 266.

50. Ibid., 267.

Chapter Four

1. Chester Gillis, *Pluralism:A New Paradigm for Theology* (Grand Rapids: Wm. B. Eerdmans, 1993), 121.

2. Charles E. Truax and Robert R. Carkhuff, *Toward Effective Counseling and Psychotherapy* (Chicago: Aldine Publishing Co., 1967).

3. Ibid., 329.

4. Ibid., 142.

5. Ibid.

6. Ibid.

7. Ibid., 285.

8. Scott Peck, *The Road Less Traveled* (New York: Simon and Schuster, 1978), 118.

9. Truax and Carkhuff, 142.

10. Ibid., 143.

11. Ibid.

12. We should note that as women are becoming more free to come forth with their tales of woe, we are discovering the vast extent to which male psychotherapists have used the privacy of their offices to exploit women clients sexually. Reports are coming from many quarters. The cover of *Newsweek*, April 13, 1992, reads "Sex and Psychotherapy." The lead article states, "Doctors Sleeping with Patients a Growing Crisis of Ethical Abuse." Even big names in the field of psychotherapy have been involved in the exposé. Barbara Noel and Kathryn Watterson in their recent book *You Must Be Dreaming* (New York: Simon and Schuster, 1992), record how they were sexually abused by Abraham Maslow, whose name is synonymous with the best in psychotherapy. They have won a damage suit in court. Certainly the psychotherapeutic encounter at the human level can be demonic.

13. Ibid., 174.

14. Ibid., 161.

15. Ibid.

16. Ibid., 26.

17. E. B. Green, *The Meaning of Salvation* (Philadelphia: The Westminster Press, 1965), 239.

18. Peck, 149.

19. Truax and Carkhuff, 177.

20. David Roberts, *Psychotherapy and a Christian View of Man* (New York: Charles Scribner's Sons, 1950).

21. Roberts, 33.

22. Ibid., 36.

23. Ibid., 37.

24. Ibid., 135.

25. Ibid.

26. Ibid., 50.

27. Ibid., 135.

28. Ibid.

29. Ibid., 129.

30. Ibid., 130.

31. Ibid., 130–131.
32. E. Stanley Jones, *Is the Kingdom of God Realism?* (New York: Abingdon, 1940), *The Word Became Flesh* (New York: Abingdon Press, 1963), and *The Way* (New York: Abingdon Press, 1946). See chapter one, pages 20ff above.
33. Roberts, 133.
34. Ibid., 51.
35. William Barclay, *The Gospel of John*, vol. 1 (Philadelphia: The Westminster Press, 1975), 62.
36. Barclay, 63.

Chapter Five

1. Jacques Dupuis, *Toward a Christian Theology of Religious Pluralism* (Maryknoll, N.Y.: Orbis Books, 1997). Dupuis and others (mostly Roman Catholic theologians) place high priority on these efforts.
2. Raymundo Pannikar, *The Unknown Christ of Hinduism* (London: Darton, Longman, and Todd, 1964).
3. Lesslie Newbigin, *The Open Secret* (Grand Rapids: Wm. B. Eerdmans Publishing Co., 1978), 197.
4. Hendrik Kraemer, *Why Christianity of All Religions?* (Philadelphia: The Westminster Press, 1962), 115. This statement by Kraemer makes abundantly clear that Gillis totally misunderstands the position I am representing here

when he says that "it is increasingly difficult to consider Christianity as the only or the vastly superior way to the divine." (Pluralism, p. 27.) This is not what the evangelical Christian who is fair-minded is saying.
5. It is true that the human person in the present life expresses herself/himself through the physical body. But the body cannot be a "part" of the person. The person is an indivisible unity and can have no "parts." Neither is a person *per se* dependent on the body. This can be seen in the scientific studies of extra-sensory perception (at Duke University and elsewhere). It is also made clear when we realize that the person will have a new and different body in the resurrection, but be the same person.
6. Cobb, 19.

Chapter Six

1. A religious institution common to India. The word comes from the Sanskrit, *A* ("away from") and *shram* ("hard work.") It is a spiritual retreat, usually held in the forest or some other remote place, led by a religious leader or "holy man."
2. *Time/Life* film by this title.
3. E. Stanley Jones, *The Christ of the Indian Road* (New York: Abingdon Press, 1925), 11.
4. Dr. Berg is a retired Lutheran minister in Minneapolis,

Minnesota. He has held many prominent positions in the Lutheran Church of America and was for many years a close associate of Stanley Jones. He is a permanent member of the Board of Directors of United Christian Ashrams International, a ministry which Dr. Jones founded.

5. E. Stanley Jones, *Christ at the Round Table* (Nashville: Abingdon Press, 1928), 21, and *The Word Became Flesh* (Nashville: Abingdon Press, 1963), 362.

6. White, Andrew, *A History of the Warfare Of Science with Theology in Christendom* (New York: Appleton, 1908).

7. Michael Barnes, *Christian Identity and Religious Pluralism* (New York: Abingdon Press, 1989).

8. Barnes, 59.

9. Ibid., 138.

10. Charles W. Foreman, "Christian Dialogues with Other Faiths,"

Toward the 21st Century in Christian Mission, James M. Phillips and Robert T. Coote, eds., (Grand Rapids: William B. Eerdmans Publishing Co., 1993), 338.

11. Jones, *Christ at the Round Table,* 50–51.

12. Ibid.

13. *Transformation*, vol. 28:1 (1993), 4–5.

14. Jones, *Christ at the Round Table,* 295.

15. E. Stanley Jones, *The Divine Yes* (New York: Abingdon Press, 1975), 66.

16. Harvey G. Cox, "Many Mansions or One Way? The Crisis in Interfaith Dialogue," *The Christian Century* 105:73, 1–5, 17–24, August 1988.

17. Ibid.

18. Ibid.

19. E. Stanley Jones, *Gandhi, Portrayal of a Friend* (Nashville: Abingdon Press, 1948).